A Pictorial History of

The University of Georgia

F. N. Boney
8 December 2000
Athens, Georgia

A Pictorial History of

The University of Georgia

Second Edition

F. N. BONEY

The University of Georgia Press   Athens

To the University of Georgia's students,
past, present, and future

© 1984, 2000 by the University of Georgia Press
Athens, Georgia 30602

Designed by Sandra Strother Hudson
Set in Baskerville

The paper in this book meets the guidelines for
permanence and durability of the Committee on
Production Guidelines for Book Longevity of the
Council on Library Resources.

Printed in the United States of America
Second Edition

04   03   02   01   00   C   5   4   3   2   1

Library of Congress Cataloging-in-Publication Data
Boney, F. N.
A pictorial history of the University of Georgia / F. N.
Boney.—2nd ed.
p.   cm.
Includes bibliographical references (p.   ) and index.
ISBN 0-8203-2198-2 (alk. paper)
1. University of Georgia—History. 2. Univeristy of Georgia—
History—Pictorial works.
I. Title: Univeristy of Georgia. II. Title.

LD1983 .B6 2000
378.758'18—dc21   99-049011

Unless otherwise indicated, the illustrations in this book
are from the Special Collections Division of the University
of Georgia Libraries. The author and the publisher
gratefully acknowledge their cooperation in the
publication of this volume.

Contents

Foreword

When you add to the University of Georgia's beautiful north campus both the vibrant research of south campus and the energy of the newly developed fine arts and recreational facilities on east campus, the sum is an amazing portrait of a dynamic educational institution. The University of Georgia continues to grow and thrive in response to the demands of a rapidly changing society.

No one charts that evolution with more clarity, detail, and affection than Professor F. N. Boney. In 1985, the University of Georgia celebrated the two hundredth anniversary of its chartering. Ancient by American standards, the proud old school sponsored numerous events and projects, including the first edition of Dr. Boney's *A Pictorial History of the University of Georgia,* published by the University of Georgia Press. Dr. Boney, a professor of history at the university at the time the first edition was published, had long been noted for his scholarship in southern and Civil War history, particularly for his work related to his native state of Virginia and his adopted state of Georgia. The first edition added the university to his list of specialties. Dr. Boney has also published many short articles on various aspects of the institution's history and a second book about the school, *A Walking Tour of the University of Georgia* (University of Georgia Press, 1989).

This new edition of *A Pictorial History of the University of Georgia* presents his original work on the university updated for the turn of the new century. The new section covers only fifteen years, but what a dramatically successful time it has been! The sudden emergence of east campus is visible evidence of boom times for the university. New buildings have crowded into the old north and south campuses, too, while enrollment has surged from 25,000 to 31,000. Individual faculty members and students have won increasing national and international recognition. Our athletic teams, always important in "Bulldog Country," boast an impressive collection of successes, highlighted recently by the strong performances of our women's teams. The Olympic events of 1996, especially the final rounds of men's and women's soccer, showcased for the world a well-organized, expanding American university running smoothly. Perhaps most often noted by visitors, a major landscaping program has made the entirety of our campus reflect the pride which Georgians take in their institution.

The dramatic progress of these fifteen years spans the final years of the long administration of Fred C. Davison, the one-year term of Henry King Stanford, the decade-long administration of Charles B. Knapp, and the early years of my leadership. But these successes, it must be noted, rest in the efforts of countless individuals in the university community—faculty, students, staff, and administrators—who worked and studied on each of the campuses, new and old, north, south, and east. I believe, however, that the people of Georgia are due the ultimate credit, for willingly, indeed eagerly, investing in their schools and colleges, especially the flagship institution in Athens.

Recent dramatic success is built on two centuries of strife and struggle, often against discouraging odds. As I walk the paths of north campus, I think of Abraham Baldwin and Josiah Meigs of Yale, who planted the seed in the wilderness; Andrew A. Lipscomb, who nurtured it during the bleak years of the Civil War and Reconstruction; Walter B. Hill, who literally and figuratively pushed the old school into the twentieth century; Harmon W. Caldwell and O. C. Aderhold, who skillfully rode the rising tide of prosperity that started as early as World War II; and many other leaders whose names may be less familiar. Georgia continues to send this institution its best and brightest young people, the next generation of leadership for the university and the state.

The saga continues as the University of Georgia enters its third century. To the many who have steered this university to a place of prominence, we give our heartfelt thanks. To those who cherish our campus, alumni and friends alike, we offer the story of its progress. This volume is your invitation—come to Athens, walk the shady paths of north campus, and share in the evolving beauty of this place.

Michael F. Adams, President
The University of Georgia

Preface

This volume presents the story of the nation's first chartered state university in words and illustrations. Looking back through the school's past was frustrating at times because old shadows sometimes refused to yield their secrets. But for the most part it was enjoyable and even fascinating to watch a little school on the frontier first struggle to survive and then gradually, over generations, evolve from a small college into one of the nation's huge modern universities. Every citizen of the state can take pride in the University of Georgia, but those of us who have been on campus as students, professors, or employees should be especially heartened. The story of the university over two hundred years is an epic that reveals that the efforts and sacrifices of earlier generations have not been in vain. Those who have been at Georgia for a generation can attest to the acceleration of progress, and those of us who are on campus now can look forward to sharing the benefits of continued growth.

Help in telling this story has come from so many sources that I can only acknowledge the assistance of major supporters. Many of the illustrations come from the Special Collections Division of the University of Georgia Libraries, where Vesta Gordon, Robert M. Willingham, Jr., John C. Edwards, and their staff gave me every assistance. John R. Stephens and his staff at the Instructional Resources Center and Marvin Sexton and his assistants in Photographic Services at the Main Library were helpful too. R. Barry Wood and Larry B. Dendy of the Public Relations Office were very generous with their resources, and the skill of Walker P. Montgomery, III, at copying old photographs was essential. Susan Barrow Tate (formerly of Special Collections) and my colleagues Kenneth Coleman and Thomas G. Dyer helped repeatedly. And the university itself, through its administrative officers, gave me the resources to complete the first edition in time for the bicentennial of the University of Georgia.

Finally, thanks are due to the Manuscript Division, South Caroliniana Library, University of South Carolina, for permission to quote from the June 23, 1835, letter from G. W. Cooper to Thomas C. Law (Thomas C. Law Papers) and from the diary of Edward Spann Hammond, July 23, 1854; to the Georgia Department of Archives and History for permission to quote from the diary of Charles Bemington King, April 15, 1843; to the Virginia Historical Society for permission to quote from the July 12, 1904, letter from Willis H. Bocock to J. H. C. Bagby (Bagby Papers); and to the Special Collections Division, University of Georgia Libraries, for permission to quote from Colonel Delony's letter of September 5, 1863, and John A. Wright's letter of January 18, 1904 (both in the William G. Delony Papers).

In 2000, the book was updated and expanded. Special thanks are due to Claude Felton and his aides in the Athletic Association; Christie Purks, Etta Roberts, and Fran Lane at the Visitors Center; Gilbert Head at the Hargrett Library; Thomas G. Dyer, associate provost; David Des Jardines at the University of Georgia Press; and the staff at University Communications, especially Tom Jackson, Larry B. Dendy, Rick O'Quinn, Paul Efland, Tori Bauer, and Peter Frey.

The Early Years,
1784–1860

The Revolutionary War ended when General Charles Cornwallis surrendered at Yorktown in the fall of 1781, but the peace treaty recognizing American independence was not signed until late in 1783. It took even longer for Georgia to recover fully from the war. Augusta and Savannah had known the humiliation of enemy occupation, and in the thinly settled back country rebels and loyalists had cut and slashed back and forth through the wilderness, moving with the flow of the fortunes of war. Georgia, the last of the original thirteen colonies, had been settled only forty years before the war, and at the end of the Revolution the state could claim barely eighty-two thousand inhabitants, more than a third of whom were slaves.

From the colony's beginning in 1733, its founders had talked vaguely about a college in the wilderness, and a few decades later the evangelist George Whitefield had dreamed of making his Bethesda School a real college, but nothing came of either idea. Indeed, in the whole prerevolutionary South there was just one college, William and Mary, and even the more advanced North had only a handful, led by Yale and Harvard. But the vigorous liberalism of the American Revolution stimulated education everywhere. In February 1784, only five months after independence, Governor Lyman Hall, a New Englander and a graduate of Yale, persuaded the Georgia legislature to grant forty thousand acres of land to endow a "college or seminary of learning." Since the new state of Georgia claimed territory all the way to the Mississippi River, the gift was not particularly generous, but it opened the way for Abraham Baldwin to establish the University of Georgia.

Baldwin, like Hall, was a graduate of Yale; after becoming a minister he taught there for several years. During the Revolutionary War he served as a chaplain, and after the war he became a lawyer. Early in 1784 he joined many other New Englanders seeking success in Georgia, where he prospered as a lawyer and politician. The ablest of Georgia's three delegates to the Constitutional Convention of 1786, he represented his state in the House and Senate until his death in 1807. Baldwin probably assisted Governor Hall in gaining the initial land grant in 1784, and after studying the document that had established Yale in 1745, he wrote a charter for Georgia. On January 25, 1785, the legislature approved the document, and the University of Georgia became the first chartered state university in the nation.

This charter presented a sweeping educational program. The plan resembled Thomas Jefferson's earlier ideas, which were not seriously attempted in Virginia until 1819: it called for a broad system of public education that would include elementary schools, academies, and a university. The entire system was given a unique plan of government designed to give the state ultimate control, but it was too complicated. The Board of Visitors included the governor, all state senators, all superior court judges, and a few other public officials; the Board of Trustees was a body of fourteen appointed members that soon became self-perpetuating. These two boards combined to form the Senatus Academicus of the University of Georgia. Within this maze only the Board of Trustees was compact enough to function, and gradually it began to assume control.

Baldwin, who had been appointed president of the system, faced enormous difficulties. The state was still undeveloped and underpopulated. Only a few private academies actually operated, and no college of any sort existed. The trustees' major asset was the land set aside by the 1784 grant; but real estate was cheap, and after a border dispute with South Carolina and further administrative confusion, the board never controlled more than about twenty thousand acres. The trustees did the best they could, selling, renting, and (hardest of all) collecting payments in a rough-and-tumble real-estate market. Nevertheless, it took years to raise enough money for the university to open its doors.

Finally, by the turn of the century, more than six thousand dollars had accumulated, and the Senatus Academicus in one of its rare sessions appointed a five-man committee to find a suitable site in the thinly settled interior of the state. Baldwin headed the group, which included John Milledge, a native Georgian and a hero of the Revolution. Milledge had very little formal education, but he would be the next governor, and consequently his support was almost as crucial as Baldwin's.

In the summer of 1801, with the assistance of a local entrepreneur named Daniel Easley, the committee selected a stretch of high, wooded ground on the west bank of the Oconee River that belonged to Easley. Milledge bought the 633 hilltop acres and immediately gave the tract, called Cedar Shoals, to the Senatus Academicus. Only 37 acres of it remained intact as the old campus. The rest became an endowment that the trustees could rent or sell in tracts to get the new school through hard times, and soon a town emerged on this land.

Baldwin, now a United States senator, had already resigned the presidency of the school and had chosen Josiah Meigs as his successor. Meigs had been Baldwin's student at Yale and, like Baldwin, had stayed on to teach there. When he reached Cedar Shoals in 1801 he found almost as many Indians as whites. The tiny village of Watkinsville was several miles away, and the immediate area around the prospective campus had only a few rude houses and a small mill owned (of course) by Daniel Easley. Acting as the school's president and sole professor, Meigs recruited a handful of students from the state's few academies and probably held classes under the trees in the fall of 1801. The next year the slowly growing student body met in a twenty-foot-square, one-and-a-half-story log cabin built for less than two hundred dollars, and Meigs and his family moved into the official president's house (built by Easley). A wooden frame grammar school was also built, because many of the new students were unprepared for college work, and the following year work began on a large three-story brick building patterned after Connecticut Hall at Yale University.

Meigs also brought the conservative Yale curriculum with him to backwoods Georgia. He saw to it that the University of Georgia copied Yale as best it could with a classical course of study that emphasized Greek and Latin. Meigs's own specialty was mathematics, which had been a part of classical education since the time of Plato, but he was also fascinated by the new science emerging in the Western world. Encouraged by his friend Thomas Jefferson, who later carried innovation much further with his elective system at the University of Virginia, Meigs added some of this modern science to the early program at the new university. Indeed, one of his first official acts was to order from London "philosophical [scientific] apparatus and a small selection of books." Meigs, a tireless measurer and quantifier, had introduced a little new learning in Georgia, and scientific studies took root at the university, to flower later in better times.

Meigs proudly presided over the first commencement in 1804. Among the nine graduates was Augustin S. Clayton, who in 1829 constructed a successful textile plant on the Oconee River a few miles away from the college. Considerable other light industry followed in the thriving town that grew up alongside the university. The old name of Cedar Shoals, hinting at the location of mills like Easley's and later Clayton's, at the very beginning gave way to the name Athens, which clearly reflected the importance of the university. The first plat (1804) projected Athens as an extension of the university with two rows of empty lots facing the campus across what would become Front Street (later Broad Street).

3

State of Georgia.   467

By the honorable John Houstoun Esquire Captain General Governor and Commander in Chief in and over the said State.

To all to whom these presents shall come Greeting:

Know Ye, that in pursuance of an Act of the General Assembly passed on the twenty fifth day of February one thousand seven hundred and eighty four and by virtue of the powers in me vested. I have by and with the advice and consent of the Honorable the Executive Council given and Granted, and by these presents in the name and behalf of the said State, Do give and Grant unto the following persons in trust, and as a public body constituted by the said Act of Assembly for the purpose of erecting and endowing a colledge or seminary of learning in the said State. That is to say, unto his Honor the Governor for the time being, and John Houstoun, James Habersham, William Few, Joseph Clay, Abraham Baldwin, William Houstoun, and Nathan Brownson, Esquires, Trustees nominated in the said Act, and to their Successors in office forever, under and agreeable to the directions of the said Law, and the future regulations of the Legislature, All that tract or parcel of land Containing five thousand acres, situate, lying and being, in the County of Franklin in the said State, and butting and bounding on all sides by vacant land, having such shape form and marks as appear by a plat of the same hereunto annexed: Together with all and Singular the rights members and appurtenances thereof whatsoever to the said tract or parcel of land belonging or in any wise appertaining, To Have and to Hold the said Tract or parcel of land and all and Singular the premises aforesaid with their and every of their rights, members and appurtenances unto the said trustees, and to their successors in office as aforesaid and to and for the use and behoof of the Public in manner before set forth, and as shall be agreeable to Law and the intent and meaning of the said Trust for ever.

Given under my hand in Council and the great Seal of the said State at this Twenty first day of September in the Year of our Lord one thousand seven hundred and eighty four and in the Ninth Year of American Independence.

Signed by his Honor the Governor in Council the 21st September 1784

J. Houstoun

Wm Freeman D.C.C.

Registered 24th Sept. 1784

A year before the chartering of the University of Georgia the state legislature set aside forty thousand acres of land as an endowment for "a college or seminary of learning." The original survey in the state records describes a five-thousand-acre lot in Franklin County in north Georgia. This tract did not become the home of the university, but it was part of the endowment of fertile soil that would soon nurture the infant school much as federal land grants would nurture American universities almost a century later. (Courtesy of the Surveyor General Department, Office of Secretary of State of Georgia.)

4

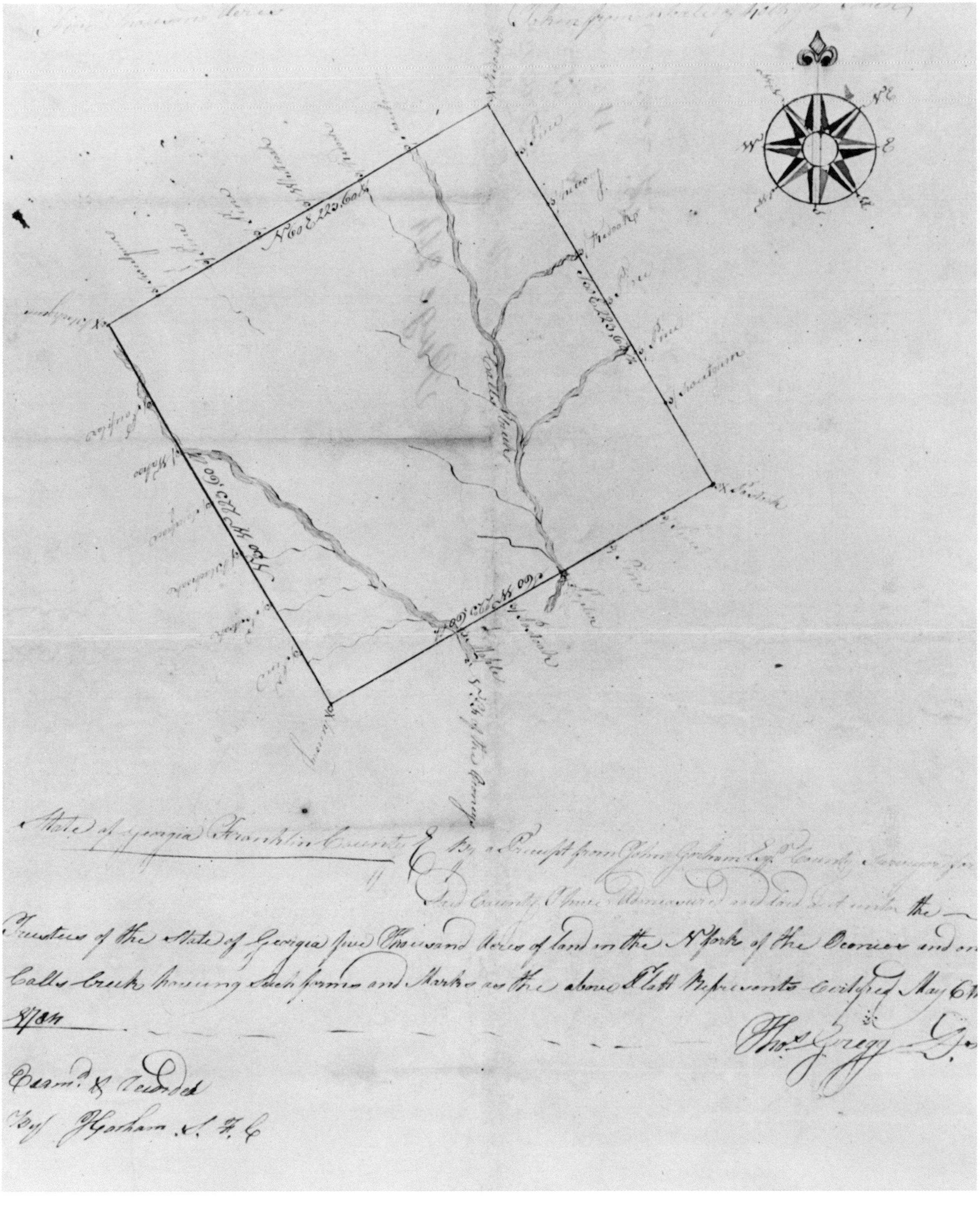

State of Georgia Franklin County ... by a Precept from John Gorham Esq. County Surveyor for

said County I have Measured and Laid out unto the

Trustees of the State of Georgia five Thousand Acres of land on the N Forks of the Oconee and on

Calls Creek having Such forms and Marks as the above Platt Represents Certified May 6th

1784

Thos. Gregg S.

Exam'd & Recorded

Jas. J Gorham S. F. C.

5

6

Facing page: Abraham Baldwin, first president of the university. A native of Connecticut, a graduate of Yale and a teacher there, a lawyer and a minister, Baldwin moved to Georgia after serving as a chaplain in the revolutionary army. Rising rapidly in law and politics, he served in the state legislature, the Confederation Congress, the Constitutional Convention of 1786, the House of Representatives, and the Senate. During his service in the state legislature he probably assisted in gaining the original land grant for a college in 1784, and the next year he wrote the charter for the University of Georgia. He served on the Board of Trustees and on the committee that decided on the location of the university. By the time the college was ready to open in 1801 Baldwin was busy in national politics, so he turned the presidency over to his friend Josiah Meigs, also from Yale. Painting by Charles Frederick Naegele (1857–1944). (Courtesy of the Georgia Museum of Art.)

Above: The university's charter, signed by Joseph Habersham, speaker of the one-house legislature, bears no date, but the legislative journal clearly indicates that it was approved in January 1785. As the years passed the charter disappeared somewhere in the state records in Atlanta, but in 1961 it was finally found in a closet among a batch of discarded documents. Now safely stored in the Special Collections Division of the University of Georgia Libraries, it symbolizes the beginning of a grand experiment deep in the backwoods of early Georgia.

Meigs concentrated his energies on the campus, where progress was steady at first. By 1806 seventy students attended the college and another forty studied at the Grammar School. Also, the first permanent brick building was completed and named Franklin College (now Old College), and a second professor arrived from Yale to teach Greek and Latin, giving Meigs more time for mathematics and science. The president took primary responsibility for the freshmen and seniors ("senior sophisters," to be exact), and his new colleague watched over the sophomores and "junior sophisters." In 1806 Meigs hired Monsieur Petit de Clairville to teach French. A liberal Jeffersonian like Meigs naturally admired France, where a great revolution had created a new society, but the study of a modern, living language was relatively new in American higher education. The Frenchman stayed only a few years, but he did begin a tenuous but persistent French affiliation at the university.

Under Meigs the University of Georgia rose from virgin soil and began to grow and to compete with other southeastern state universities. The University of North Carolina was chartered four years after Georgia, but it actually began operations six years earlier at Chapel Hill, a remote interior spot much like Cedar Shoals. South Carolina, which had dominated Georgia in the colonial period, chartered a state university in 1801 and opened it in 1805, copying much of the Georgia system. Despite Thomas Jefferson's entreaties, conservative Virginia waited until 1819 to establish its university.

On July 25, 1801, the Augusta Chronicle informed the reading public that the Senatus Academicus had chosen a site for the university, "an institution deeply interesting to the present age, and still more to an encreasing posterity." Two columns to the right of the announcement is a notice about a runaway slave, and one column to the left is the latest news from Europe.

In the North, church-related colleges like Harvard and Yale dominated, and in 1819 Dartmouth went all the way to the United States Supreme Court to defend its original charter and frustrate an attempted takeover by the state of New Hampshire. The South was free of entrenched church schools and open for the development of state universities like Georgia. But if the churches did not at first establish rival colleges, they did attack from within. In Athens President Meigs, an opinionated Yankee, clashed with Hope Hull, an abrasive southerner on the Board of Trustees. Nicknamed "Broad-

9

Josiah Meigs became the second president of the University of Georgia in 1800. He established the university along the lines of his alma mater, Yale, and he added an emphasis on science that remained long after his tenure. Meigs, an outspoken Jeffersonian liberal, eventually clashed with the conservative trustees. He resigned the presidency in 1810, and the following year he resigned his professorship of science and mathematics and moved back to the North, where he died in 1822. This portrait was painted by Lewis Gregg in 1831. (Courtesy of the Georgia Museum of Art.)

axe" by his awed Methodist congregation, Hull established the first church in Athens and became the first of a long line of critics who over two centuries denounced godlessness and debauchery at the University of Georgia.

More important, Hull was head of the Prudential Committee, a kind of executive subcommittee of the Board of Trustees made up of the trustees living around Athens who could exercise some day-to-day supervision of the school. This committee steadily gained influence as the

Board of Trustees grew to almost thirty members before the Civil War, and Hull did not hesitate to use the committee's power in the name of the Lord. After all, the university was modeled after Yale, a Congregational school, and its charter conceded the importance of "religion and morality." The state of Georgia had at least its share of sinners, but the Methodists and Baptists and Presbyterians were on the march, determined to get rid of the free-thinking (and free-speaking) Meigs and bring the

| No. D. Coltram | No. 12 Morris | No. 13 Morris | No. 14 Morris | No. 15 Allan | | No. 16 Allan | No. 17 Douglas | | No. 18 Lewis | No. 19 Going | No. 20 Hays | | No. 21 Cary | No. 2 Cary |
| No. B. | No. 11 Phinizy | No. 10 Phinizy | No. 9 Phinizy | No. 8 Meigs | | No. 7 Allan | No. 6 Martin | | No. 5 Wright | No. 4 Thurman | No. 3 Thomas | | No. 2 McKigney | No. 1 Phin |

PLAN of part of the Lots laid off in Athens,
ordered to be recorded, May 31, 1805

In 1803 the legislature authorized the University of Georgia to survey lots for sale while retaining thirty-seven acres for the campus. This plat or map, drawn in 1804, was recorded in May 1805 and entered in the official minutes of the Board of Trustees. The only university buildings are the President's House, the wooden Grammar School, and the main brick "College" building (the word old seems to have been added later). The building to the right presumably belonged to Hope Hull. The numbered lots represent the future town of Athens, but at this time neither Front (later Broad) nor Clayton streets had been named. The entrepreneur Ferdinand Phinizy owned many of these lots, and President Josiah Meigs bought lot number 8.

slightly unorthodox university to heel. In 1808 Hull not only built a small wooden chapel on campus but persuaded the university to put up most of the money for it. The stage was being set for a change in leadership.

President Meigs had as much trouble with the trustees over politics as over religion. He was too liberal for the trustees, whom he dismissed as "a damned pack or a band of Tories and speculators" while hinting at shady dealings with the school's funds. Meigs irritated a lot of people, and the whole school began to suffer. By 1810 only twenty-five students remained in the Franklin College building and another fifteen at the Grammar School. Denounced by the trustees for "great misconduct," Meigs resigned as president the next year, and in 1812 he also gave up his professorship of science and mathematics. After sarcastically offering to stay on as the bell ringer, he moved his family back to the North and finally settled in as a professor of

11

12

Facing page, above: Old College (1806), modeled after Connecticut Hall at Yale, is the oldest standing structure in the Athens area. Although some early classes were held there, it served mainly as a dormitory for over a century; it had forty-eight bedrooms but only twenty-four fireplaces. By the beginning of the twentieth century the original Georgia bricks were crumbling and needed to be replaced. Chancellor Walter B. Hill prepared to demolish Old College as he modernized the university, but an early effort at historic preservation saved the old structure. Given a new brick skin, it continued to serve as a dormitory. During World War II the navy extensively renovated the interior and used the building as a barracks for its preflight school. This photograph, taken about 1875, is from Davis's Souvenir Album.

Facing page, below: Philosophical Hall, the second oldest surviving structure on campus, was completed in 1821. At first it housed books and scientific equipment, but over the years it has been a classroom building, a gymnasium, a boardinghouse, the College of Agriculture, the home of Registrar Thomas W. Reed, a snack bar, and the office of the University of Georgia Press. In the 1950s it was renamed to honor President Moses Waddel, and since 1977 it has been known as the Dean Rusk Center for International Law. This photograph was taken early in the twentieth century.

Above: The Demosthenian Literary Society was organized in 1803, and its meeting hall was constructed in 1824 at a cost of four thousand dollars. Demosthenian Hall also housed a considerable library. The antebellum students' after-class activities centered in this society or its rival, the Phi Kappa Literary Society. When this photograph was taken around 1875, Demosthenian Hall looked much the same as it did in the antebellum era.

"experimental philosophy" at Columbian College (now George Washington University), where he died in 1852. Meigs had done his best, and he would soon be missed.

The foundering college selected as Meigs's successor the Reverend John Brown of South Carolina. This began the century-long custom of appointing Protestant ministers to the presidency, and until just before the Civil War the Presbyterians maintained a monopoly. Brown hung on for five dreary years while the university withered, forgotten by the people and neglected by the legislature. Even rumors (which turned out to be false) of an Indian attack during the War of 1812 could barely stir the lethargic campus to action. Finally, in 1817, Brown was replaced by the Reverend Robert Finley, a graduate and a trustee of Princeton College and a founder of the American Colonization Society. Finley found barely two dozen students left and "the buildings nearly in a state of ruins." He plunged into his work, but died of typhus two months later.

For a time it seemed that the university would die with him. Several prominent men declined the presidency before the position was accepted by the Reverend Moses Waddel (pronounced like *model* until the next generation added another *l*). The university desperately needed strong leadership, and Waddel provided it. A precocious child of the Scot-Irish frontier in North Carolina, young Waddel was well educated in rural academies and at age fourteen began teaching in similar schools. A few years later in Georgia, he experienced a religious conversion and enrolled at Hampden-Sydney, a struggling Presbyterian college in Virginia. He received his A.B. in 1791 and was ordained a minister. For years he operated the highly successful Willington Academy in backwoods South Carolina, which educated many prominent men like William H. Crawford, Augustus B. Longstreet, and John C. Calhoun (whose sister Waddel married). Waddel impressed almost everyone, but many observers predicted that he would be the last president of the university. When he arrived in 1819 the school was, in Waddel's own words, "nearly extinct, consisting of only seven students with three professors."

As much a preacher as an educator, Waddel continued the work Hope Hull had begun.

Meigs's innovations were never entirely eliminated, but the University of Georgia did become more academically orthodox and much more religiously oriented; indeed, under Waddel it increasingly resembled small church schools like his alma mater, Hampden-Sydney. Waddel was a man with a mission. He established the First Presbyterian Church in Athens, and he also built a small Presbyterian church right on the campus on Front Street where the Academic Building now stands. A few years later the Baptists built a wooden chapel on the northwestern corner of the campus (now the corner of Lumpkin and Broad). Hull's original wooden chapel on campus had been dismantled by this time, and the Methodists did not replace it.

Working tirelessly, Waddel traveled all over the state recruiting new students and soon built enrollment up to a hundred. When free-spirited sons of well-to-do Georgians reached the campus, they quickly discovered that they had entered a new world. Waddel expected his staff of four professors and two tutors to work very hard, and he expected the same of the students. He also demanded strict obedience to authority. Even the wildest and most rambunctious students met their match in "Old Pewt," who, when really riled, banished proud collegians to the lowly Grammar School, the worst fate short of expulsion. Indeed, Waddel never hesitated to expel unruly students. Robert Toombs, for example, lasted three years at the university, breaking every rule in the book and then arguing eloquently for one more chance, but finally he departed, claiming that he resigned a split second before President Waddel could expel him. In 1822 Donald McIntosh was "sent away" (as Waddel put it), and, as frequently happened in such cases, the president then had to face McIntosh's angry parents. But "Old Pewt" always documented his cases and stood his ground. He carefully listed McIntosh's liquor bills at six different stores in Athens to substantiate the charge of "habitual intemperance" and firmly rejected the family's entreaties. When stern, efficient Moses Waddel "sent away" students, they stayed away.

Waddel's administrative talents were even more useful in financial matters. Just four years

Moses Waddel became president of the University of Georgia in 1819. The school had all but collapsed when Waddel arrived, but in the ten years of his administration he raised its enrollment from no more than seven students to a steady one hundred. He imposed strict discipline, insisted on high academic standards, and brought his stern Presbyterianism into the daily lives of the students. He recruited better students and coaxed more money out of the legislature. When he resigned the presidency in 1829 to return to the ministry, the university was in sound shape. This portrait is probably by George Cooke.

before his arrival the state legislature finally decided to start giving the beleagured university some sort of consistent financial support. The original land grant of 1784 had never been productive, so the trustees were authorized to sell what was left of it. The proceeds were used to buy bank stock that yielded annual interest of around eight thousand dollars. The legislature guaranteed this annual return and eventually assumed it as a permanent state obligation. Thus when Waddel arrived in 1819 the university finally had a steady if limited source of state funds which it could count on to supplement tuition payments, proceeds from the sale or rental of parcels of the Milledge grant in

Athens, and gifts from private benefactors (rare in those days).

The legislature also began to appropriate more funds for building. The campus looked run down in 1819 when Waddel received President James Monroe, who was touring the nation, but in 1821 the legislators appropriated twenty thousand dollars for the construction of another large brick building. By 1823 the four-story structure, known as New College, was completed. Waddel also built a much smaller two-story brick building designed to house the school's more than two thousand books and its scientific equipment and also to serve as a cha-

A native of Vermont and a graduate of Middlebury College, Alonzo Church moved to the South and married into a planter family. He came to the university to teach mathematics in 1819, and ten years later he assumed the presidency when Waddel resigned. He held the post for thirty years, a school record. Always a stern traditionalist, Church became more rigid and irritable in his later years. But when he finally resigned in 1859, the citizens of Athens gave him a fine silver service to honor his years with the university.

pel. Originally called Philosophical Hall, it was renamed Waddel Hall in the 1950s, and today it is called the Rusk Center. In 1824 the Demosthenian Literary Society, founded in 1803, erected its own two-story building just north of Hull's battered old wooden chapel. In 1829 the old Grammar School was torn down as the age of admission was raised from thirteen to sixteen.

The university's slow progress reflected the much more vigorous growth of the whole state. By 1830 Georgia's population had soared to over half a million people, including 220,000 black slaves. The western boundary had moved east to the Chattahoochee River, but Georgia was still the largest state east of the Mississippi. All Indians had been removed except the Cherokees in the northwestern corner of the state, and they would soon trek west too. Small towns like Athens, Eatonton, Thomasville, Washington, and the capital at Milledgeville flourished as the rural population thickened in the prosperous cotton belt, and soon vigorous new cities like Macon, Columbus, and Atlanta would challenge Augusta and Savannah. Georgia was maturing rapidly, and though no statewide public school system began to develop until the late 1850s, many private academies and other secondary schools had appeared, which meant that the university could concentrate on higher education.

Waddel had seen that the University of Georgia moved forward with the state, but by 1829 he was ready to retire. The university was progressing steadily if not spectacularly; his work was done. He returned to South Carolina to teach and preach, but after a severe stroke in 1836 he came back to Athens to live with his son James, who taught ancient languages at the university.

Thus he could spend his last four years watching the university—in a way *his* university—continue to progress under his successor, the Reverend Alonzo Church, another staunch Presbyterian. A graduate of Middlebury College in Connecticut, Church moved to Georgia, married into the planter class, and taught at an academy in Eatonton. He came to the university the same year as Waddel as a professor of

In 1831 the Ivy Building was constructed just north of Demosthenian
Hall. It housed the university's small library until 1862, when the Library
Building was erected beside it. A corner
of the Library Building is visible in the
round photograph, which was taken in
1893. By that time the law school occupied one floor of the Ivy Building. The
photograph above, taken about 1875,
is from Davis's Souvenir Album. In
1905 the Ivy Building and the Library
Building were linked by a Corinthian
portico to form the present Academic
Building.

New College was built in 1823 to serve as a classroom and dormitory building, but it burned to the ground in 1830. Rebuilt in 1832 minus its fourth floor, the old building served the university in many capacities over the years. Now it houses the office of the dean of the Franklin College of Arts and Sciences. This photograph, taken about 1875, appeared in Davis's Souvenir Album.

mathematics. Ten years later, in 1829, he took over from Waddel and served as president for thirty consecutive years, the longest administration in the school's history.

Church generally continued Waddel's conservative policies, but he never totally eliminated Meigs's early liberal influence. In the late 1840s students still took a good bit of "natural philosophy" or science, including botany, chemistry, mineralogy, astronomy, and geology. Most of them dreaded the mathematics requirements: arithmetic, algebra, trigonometry, logarithms, and calculus as well as more practical courses in surveying, navigation, leveling, measuring, and, for a few years, civil engineering. Math

and science courses were part of the normal American collegiate curriculum by the 1840s, but Georgia still put more than average stress on these subjects.

The university also continued to require French for two terms (quarters, not semesters) and also a smattering of political economy, oratory, rhetoric, logic, moral philosophy, English literature, "Laws of Nations," and "Evidences of Christianity." In 1857 Richard Malcolm Johnston offered the first real history course, but the Civil War ended his stay at the university before he published his *Georgia Sketches, Dukesborough Tales,* and other works describing the plain folk of old Georgia with humor and affection.

A more significant innovation began in 1854

One of the school's few scholarship students, Alexander H. Stephens never received any criticism from a professor and had compiled an outstanding academic record by the time he graduated in 1832. For many years he was a Whig leader in the United States House of Representatives. Although he opposed secession at the Georgia convention in January 1861, he became vice-president of the Confederacy. Stephens, who spent much of his time criticizing President Jefferson Davis, joined with Governor Joseph E. Brown and Robert Toombs, another Georgia graduate, to obstruct many Confederate policies in Georgia. After the war he served in Congress again and won the governorship in 1882, but "Little Aleck" had long passed his political peak when he died in 1883. Always a supporter of his alma mater, he served on the Board of Trustees for many years.

when Dr. William Terrell offered to give the university twenty thousand dollars in state bonds, with the interest from these bonds paying the salary of a new professor who would give free lectures on "Agriculture as a Science; the practice and improvement of different people; on Chemistry and Geology, so far as they may be useful in Agriculture; on Manures, Analysis of Soils, and on Domestic Economy, particularly referring to the Southern States." A native of Virginia, Terrell became one of a handful of prosperous scientific planters in Hancock County. He briefly served as a congressman and a trustee of the university, and toward the end of his life made the university the most generous offer since John Milledge had given the land for the main campus in 1801. President Church and his trustees quickly accepted Terrell's offer and also his suggestion for the first professor of agriculture: "Dr. Daniel Lee, who has spent twenty years of his life in the study and practice of Agriculture, and who will bring to its duties, all his skill and a zeal that ought to ensure success." A native of New York who had become a thorough south-

erner, Lee had only a few years at the university before the Civil War intervened, but a seed had been planted that would eventually grow into an agricultural college reaching into every county of the state.

Church was realistic enough to see the need for occasional change, and in matters of curriculum Georgia was probably a little more flexible than most colleges of the period, but Church, like the great majority of American educators, was basically conservative, and Georgia students were still required to take a great deal of Greek and Latin. The classics were stressed in the freshman and sophomore years when recitation in class was emphasized, and the more innovative courses tended to appear in the junior and senior years when the professors lectured and the students took notes. Students marched through college in lock step with little encouragement of independent thought, and the whole ordeal was capped off with a final term devoted to preparation for comprehensive testing over the whole curriculum.

Church also continued Waddel's policy of cultivating the soul as well as the mind. Yale's old puritanical rules were a good beginning for a long series of regulations to make the students behave morally and properly, and by the time of Church's administration these directives covered sixteen pages of a ledger. Students had to go to chapel in the morning and evening during the week and to the church of their choice on Sunday. In true Calvinist fashion the rules of deportment stressed what was forbidden: gambling, disorderly conduct, cursing, fighting, dueling, drunkenness, card games, and billiards. Circuses were off limits, but after

Waddel dancing was not specifically forbidden. Violation of any significant state law meant expulsion. Student militia units had gotten out of hand quickly, so they were disbanded and general disarmament declared; no student could "keep any gun, pistol, Dagger, Dirk, sword cane or any other offensive weapon in his room in College or elsewhere." Students were not allowed to have a dog or riding animal on campus, nor did they bring servants to ease the burdens of campus life.

The students faced a spartan existence while university officials exercised sweeping powers over their daily lives. A few adjusted quickly and never received a reprimand or a fine. Alexander H. Stephens, one of the few scholarship students, compiled a spotless record from 1828 to 1832. He went on to serve sixteen years in the national House of Representatives and in 1861 became vice-president of the Confederacy, though he had consistently opposed secession. At the other extreme, wild young bucks like Bob Toombs were thrown out. Most Georgia students struggled to adjust and survive. The antebellum South tolerated and sometimes even encouraged an individualistic kind of personal freedom for white males, and many students found it difficult to abandon the easygoing habits of farm and plantation, but most managed to stay on, in and out of trouble, until finally liberated after four years by a bachelor of arts degree.

The regimentation was just too strict, and absolutely nothing in the way of organized athletics existed as a safety valve. Inevitably, students let off steam, violating the rules and regulations of the system. Drunkenness and disorderly conduct were the most common offenses, and fights frequently erupted, especially after evening chapel. Young Edward Spann Hammond, the proper son of the wealthy, powerful South Carolina senator James H. Hammond, mentioned these fights rather disdainfully in his diary during his junior year of 1852. In his entry for July 23 he described one that got out of hand: "The greatest gloom pervades college today. Last night Hal Pond my class-mate and a Sophomore named Humphries quarreled about a trifle when after several blows were dealt with canes Humphries stabbed Pond in the left side with his cane sword. Pond came near dying

from it in the night and now he's in a precarious state. Humphries fled about mid-day. What an awful thing!" Humphries disappeared, Pond finally recovered after lingering near death for several weeks, and Spann Hammond graduated the next year. He became a doctor, a state legislator, and later a Confederate officer, and lived well into the twentieth century.

Such bloody encounters occurred occasionally on campuses all over the country, but at Georgia (and other colleges) the overwhelming majority of disruptions involved mischievous but relatively harmless highjinks. Lectures were disrupted; fences, stairs, bells, and other equipment were stolen; dormitory rooms were raided and sacked; and town folks were harassed as students continued to devise new ways to challenge the establishment. Steward's Hall, the dining room, was a trouble spot, partly because of its regular (day in and day out) menu:

BREAKFAST: coffee and tea, corn and wheat bread, butter, bacon or beef.

DINNER: corn bread, bacon and other cuts of pork, a vegetable, another meat or poultry, molasses every other day, soup twice a week, dessert once a week.

SUPPER: coffee, tea and milk, corn and wheat bread, butter.

Students constantly complained about the food, of course, and occasionally food fights erupted, even with faculty present.

The embattled professors were the only policemen on campus. Already carrying heavy teaching loads, they resented their disciplinary duties, and some eventually rebelled. The most despised obligation, patrolling the campus in the evening, fell mostly to the unmarried professors and tutors who lived in the dormitories. Most did their duty, seeking out and reporting delinquents and then holding court to mete out punishment. Strict but consistent, they even expelled one of President Church's sons for drunkenness.

Enforcing discipline was not merely disagreeable; sometimes it was dangerous. The students' rambunctiousness never went as far at Georgia

The Chapel, built in 1832 to replace an old wooden structure, became a center of activities for the small school. *The tall cupola housed the bell that signaled class periods. It was removed in 1913 to give the old building its modern (and more purely classical)* *appearance. This photograph, from Davis's Souvenir Album, was taken about 1875.*

The Phi Kappa Literary Society was established in 1820 by Joseph Henry Lumpkin as a rival to the Demosthenians. At first meetings were held secretly in the attic of the Chapel. In 1836 Phi Kappa Hall was completed, and the rivalry with the Demosthenians intensified.

After the Civil War both societies began to decline gradually. In 1888 a gymnasium was set up on the ground floor of the building. For many years the first floor served as the office and library of E. Merton Coulter, professor of history and editor of the Georgia Historical Quarterly, *and now it is used as a*

computer training center. The large room upstairs is still used as a formal meeting room. This photograph was taken around 1900.

as at Mercer, where a faculty member was seriously wounded, or at the University of Virginia, where a professor was shot dead. Still, in 1840 six drunken seniors stoned President Church and Professor Charles F. McCay, leaving both badly bruised. McCay was an outstanding teacher but an ardent disciplinarian, and a year earlier students had slipped into his room in New College one night, carried out clothing, bedding, lecture notes—everything—and made a roaring bonfire in the middle of the campus. Undeterred, McCay continued to champion law and order on campus, and in the 1840s, as faculty secretary in charge of sending students' grades home to parents, he included a free bit of his own philosophy:

> Almost all the misconduct of students at College, may be traced either directly or indirectly to the imprudent use of money. The less money they have beyond their necessary expenses, the more secure will their characters be, and the more will they be guarded against useless extravagance, self-sufficiency, and vice. It is very desirable that all their disbursements should be made in cash, and that no running accounts be opened in the Town.

This print first appeared in Gleason's Magazine *in 1854 but probably depicts the campus about a decade earlier. On the left is Phi Kappa Hall (1834). The second building from the left is not accurately portrayed but* *probably represents Philosophical Hall (1821) or the faculty home now called the Lustrat House. In the center are Old College (1806) and New College (1832). The Chapel is shown with its bell tower, which was removed in 1913. Next to the Chapel is Demosthenian Hall (1824), and the last* *building on the right is the Ivy Building, not yet covered with ivy. At the extreme right is a corner of the Presbyterian church built by President Waddel.*

If the Son or Ward is allowed to obtain credits, we earnestly recommend, that you authorize them only to a definite and limited extent, and that all the persons concerned be notified that no debt will be paid without this authority. A faithful adherence to this rule on the part of all the Parents and Guardians would, we are persuaded, produce a most important and lasting good to the College.

This certainly did not enhance his popularity with the students. By 1850 the fiery McCay had rebelled and begun to clash with President Church. He and other professors objected to their burdensome and occasionally hazardous police duties. In 1853 McCay resigned in disgust, but, like many others who had some rough times on campus, he later gave generously to the university. His complicated bequest has now grown to a fund of one million dollars for faculty salaries.

Equally fiery William D. Wash, a graduate of 1855 who stayed on in New College as a tutor, usually held his own in scuffles with the students, but several times he was besieged in his room, which afterward looked as if it had been bombarded by artillery. Young Wash was as scrappy as his antagonists, and a few years later a comrade in the Confederate army called him "the bravest man I ever saw." Most of the faculty were gentler men, but despite setbacks and embarrassments they generally maintained reasonable control as the school moved ahead.

The most obvious sign of progress was the building boom of the 1830s. This decade and Church's presidency got off to a disastrous start in 1830 when New College caught fire in the

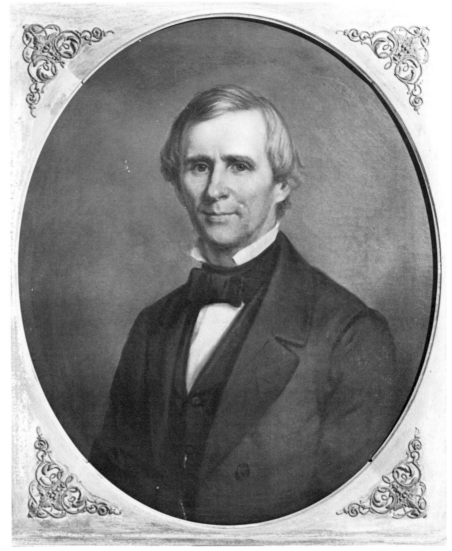

Charles F. McCay taught mathematics and civil engineering at the university in the 1840s and early 1850s and also served as faculty secretary. A strict disciplinarian, he sometimes ran into trouble with the wilder students, but everyone agreed that he was an outstanding teacher. He clashed with the autocratic President Church, and in 1855 he resigned. McCay was president of South Carolina College from 1855 to 1857, when he went into the insurance business. Like some others who had had rough times in Athens, McCay supported the university. In 1869 he donated a thousand dollars to the library, and a decade later he remembered the University of Georgia in his will. The provision was very complicated, but a century later it generated a fund of almost a million dollars to enhance faculty salaries. (Courtesy of the Office of Public Relations.)

middle of the night. All of the students escaped from their rooms, but the books and scientific equipment in the library (recently transferred from Philosophical Hall) were destroyed as the building burned to the ground.

Undeterred, President Church pushed ahead, and new buildings began to transform the old campus. By 1832 New College was rebuilt, minus its original fourth floor. The same year Hope Hull's old chapel was finally torn down, and on the site a new chapel rose. Built like a Doric Greek temple and crowned with a bell cupola, the Chapel cost fifteen thousand dollars. Today, without its awkward cupola, it remains a centerpiece of the original campus. Church also secured the construction of two faculty homes on campus for a total cost of four thousand dollars, and in 1833 he ventured almost half a mile

northwest of the campus to establish a botanical garden. Covering several acres of the original Milledge land grant north of present-day Broad Street, the garden was designed to assist in the study of natural history, but it soon became popular with townspeople as a park, and students found it a fine place for courting.

In 1831 a new library building was completed on campus between the Presbyterian church and Demosthenian Hall. Because ivy later covered the sides of this structure, it became known as the Ivy Building. Books were given by the British and American governments, former governor George R. Gilmer, the faculty, and others, and the university bought a few volumes. The number of books in this new building grew to about eighteen thousand in 1860,

Athens and the university in the 1840s. This painting by George Cooke shows the town on the horizon to the right and the university on the rise to the left. Old College, New College, and the Chapel stand clearly against the skyline. Philo-

sophical Hall and Phi Kappa Hall are a little to the right, and Demosthenian Hall and the Ivy Building are barely visible behind them. Athens had already developed some light industry like the textile mill at the middle left (now O'Malley's). The Georgia Railroad, which began at Augusta in 1834, had

reached Athens by 1841. As shown in this painting, the line just stopped, with no station or warehouse. The railroad did not bridge the Oconee River until late in the nineteenth century.

and Church ceaselessly worked to raise funds for a larger building that would include an expanded library on its second floor. Waddel's old Presbyterian church was demolished to clear the way, but Church had retired by the time the Library Building was completed in 1862 at a cost of $14,600. In 1905 this structure and the enlarged Ivy Building were joined to make the present Academic Building, and the library moved again to larger quarters.

Meanwhile, thanks to the efforts of Joseph Henry Lumpkin, private funds totaling five thousand dollars paid for the construction of another building on campus. Lumpkin, a native Athenian, had entered the University of Georgia in 1812, but when the school seemed to be on the verge of extinction he transferred to Princeton. After his graduation in 1819, he returned to Athens to practice law, and in 1820 he organized Phi Kappa, a secret literary society to rival the Demosthenians. In 1836 Phi Kappa

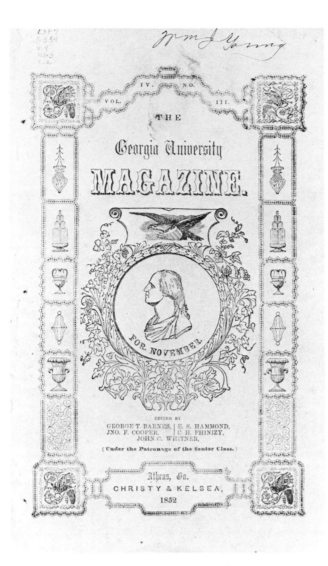

Hall arose near Front Street well north of Philosophical Hall. Each literary society built up its own private collection of books. Their four or five thousand volumes proved essential because under Waddel and Church the college library was overstocked with theological works and thin in most other areas.

Even more important, the Demosthenians and Phi Kappas gave the students a refuge from the rigid routine of the college. Most students joined one of these competing societies, which also served as social clubs with secret rituals much like the later fraternities. The intense rivalry between the two sometimes spilled over into open brawling, and some alumni carried their love of one society (and hatred of the other) right to their graves.

The students ran their own literary societies, and, accustomed to strict discipline, they drew up complicated regulations. A really unruly member could be expelled, but the usual punishment was a fine. Sleeping during meetings was a common offense, for sometimes the proceedings dragged on too long, even for the patient audiences of the antebellum era. Crawford W. Long, who is remembered today for his use of anesthesia in surgery, was once fined by the Demosthenians for falling asleep in a meeting.

Literary societies flourished at most antebellum colleges, but the Phi Kappas and Demosthenians were especially active. Their debates often attracted considerable attention, and they seldom avoided sensitive issues, even slavery. They debated and then voted on every conceivable question, but these votes were based more on the skill of the advocates than the actual issues. Briefly in 1829 the debaters unanimously denounced protective tariffs and even wore gray homespun in protest, but all over the state the pro—nullification of tariffs movement faded rapidly and the drab clothing was quickly discarded.

The literary societies at Georgia also sponsored public speeches, especially during the elaborate graduation ceremonies in August. Sometimes distinguished graduates were invited to address joint meetings of both groups. In 1835 the Phi Kappas invited the lawyer Daniel Chandler, first honor graduate of the class of 1826. Chandler's talk was routine in style and delivery—flowery by modern standards—but the content was unusual: he called for higher education for white women.

Chandler apparently was not the only Georgian who thought that women could and should be educated. The year after his speech one of the nation's first women's colleges, Georgia Female College, was established in Macon; it was taken over by the Methodists and renamed Wesleyan College in 1843. The first president of that new school was a University of Georgia alumnus, George F. Pierce (class of 1832), who later became a prominent Methodist bishop.

The Methodists also established Emory in 1836, and the Baptists opened Mercer the next year. Even the Presbyterians, who had one of their own running the University of Georgia for four decades, followed suit in 1838 with Oglethorpe College. By the 1850s the state had twenty self-proclaimed colleges, but most of these were no more than high schools or academies. Emory, Mercer, and Oglethorpe quickly developed into colleges very similar to the University of Georgia under Church, and by the 1840s they were competing vigorously with the older state university.

At the same time—and not entirely coincidentally—financial support from the state began to decline a little. Even during the building boom of the early 1830s the state had not been generous toward its university. During the next two decades its contribution was even smaller, and briefly in the 1840s the faculty shrank from six professors to four. Georgia's state government was very limited, and its main assets, the former Indian lands in the western half of the state,

were given away by lottery as family farms. In combination with traditionally low taxes on land and slaves, this liberal land policy kept the state's treasury bare and fostered a conservative attitude toward public expenditures for education.

Normally the university's annual income amounted to no more than $20,000, less than half of which came from the state. Students paid $50 tuition for an academic year of nine months, and with enrollment consistently over a hundred, this meant at least $5,000 in income. Students also paid from $100 to $140 a year for room and board, depending on accommodations, but some of this was spent off campus. The line between private and public institutions was not yet clearly drawn, and, though subject to the state's control, the University of Georgia functioned much like competing private schools in Georgia and the rest of the country. Sometimes the state gave more generous support to popular private schools like the Medical College of Georgia at Augusta than to the university itself. Georgia resembled other southern and midwestern states in its halting efforts to develop or at least encourage higher education, and the federal government remained far away in Washington with little power or influence.

On the eve of the Civil War colleges all over the nation remained small, struggling institutions. The University of Georgia held its own against Emory, Mercer, and Oglethorpe—the enrollment of all four fluctuated around 100—but it slipped behind many of the better-known schools in other states. By 1860 Harvard and Virginia both had more than 600 students. Yale had over 400, and the University of North Carolina almost as many. Even other state universities of the Deep South were moving ahead of Georgia: South Carolina with 170 students, Alabama with 137, and Mississippi with 216.

Even though the University of Georgia remained comparatively small, its alumni were a match for those of any other school in their loyalty to their alma mater. In 1834 Augustin S. Clayton (class of 1804) founded the Alumni Society, which has faithfully supported the university ever since.

Many former students did well as planters, bankers, and businessmen, and a number of prominent alumni emerged before the Civil

War. Georgia's two statues in the Hall of Fame in the nation's capitol building represent Alexander H. Stephens and Crawford W. Long, who roomed together in Old College in 1832, when Stephens was a senior and Long a fourteen-year-old freshman nicknamed "Baby." Shy and retiring all his life, Long may well be the university's most distinguished alumnus. After graduating in 1835, he enrolled at the University of Pennsylvania, where he received his M.D. in 1839. He interned in New York and then came home and settled near Athens. In 1842 he removed a tumor from the neck of a friend whom he had anesthetized with ether. Three years later he anesthetized his wife, who was giving birth to their second child; several years later Queen Victoria's doctor performed the same feat with much fanfare. By 1846 Long had performed eight operations with anesthesia. As always, he neglected to publicize his own achievements, and only much later was he recognized as a great pioneer in modern medicine.

Other Georgia alumni became writers. Francis R. Goulding (class of 1830) wrote *Robert and Harold; or, The Young Marooners on the Florida Coast,* a best seller in the 1850s, and other novels. He also constructed a sewing machine (of sorts) for his wife. Henry Timrod and Charles

Henry Smith of the class of 1847 made significant but very different contributions. Frail health and frailer finances forced Timrod to quit school after two years, but he developed into an outstanding southern poet, in his time second only to Sidney Lanier. Smith specialized in southern folk humor as a sort of nineteenth-century Will Rogers, and his newspaper columns, published from 1861 to 1903 under the pseudonym "Bill Arp," dispensed Cracker wit and wisdom.

Though often denounced as "godless," the university produced many ministers, including Bishop George F. Pierce (class of 1832) and

Benjamin M. Palmer (1838), first moderator of the Southern Association of the Presbyterian church. A few alumni became college presidents. Moses Waddel's son John N. Waddell (class of 1829) was president of the University of Mississippi and Jabez L. M. Curry of Howard College in Alabama. Curry's varied activities included several terms in the United States and Confederate congresses and service as a Baptist minister, but he is best known for his postwar crusade to educate the southern masses (male and female, black and white), which did so much to bring the South back into the main-

One of the antebellum faculty houses, called the Strahan House. Professor Charles N. Strahan, class of 1883, taught at the university for sixty-two years and lived in this house for much of that time. Professor Richard Mal- *colm Johnston, the author of* Dukesborough Tales, *lived there in the last years before the Civil War. In modern times the old house served as a student center before being destroyed in the early 1960s to make way for the new* *law library. This drawing of the Strahan House, dated Christmas 1865, is entitled "Palace of King John Lackland" and addressed "To Annie Smith, the bewitching, from her venerable cousin Arthur Huger."*

stream of American life. John LeConte (class of 1838) and his brother Joseph (1841) taught science courses at their alma mater until the middle 1850s, when they moved to South Carolina College in Columbia. During the Civil War they helped produce niter and other chemicals for the Confederate army. After the war they moved west and helped build the University of California into an outstanding school. They gained international recognition for their own work, John in medicine and physics and the more famous Joseph in optics, geology, evolutionary theory, and philosophy.

Law was the most popular profession for Georgia graduates, and many of these lawyers also prospered in politics. The university produced far more than its share of leaders, the majority of whom practiced a moderate to conservative brand of politics that appealed to the voters of Georgia—until 1861. John G. Shorter (class of 1837) became the Civil War governor of Alabama. John A. Campbell (1826) served as a justice of the United States Supreme Court from 1853 to 1861 and then became assistant secretary of war for the Confederacy. Howell

William Terrell moved from Virginia to Georgia and became one of a number of scientific farmers in Hancock County. He was a trustee of the university in the 1820s and also briefly served in Congress, but his chief interest was agriculture. In 1854, not long before his death, Terrell gave the University of Georgia twenty thousand dollars in state bonds to endow a chair of agriculture. Eighteen years before the establishment of the College of Agriculture and the Mechanic Arts and over half a century before the construction of Conner Hall, Terrell planted the first seed at the antebellum university.

Cobb—"Fatty" to his friends in the class of 1834—served ably for nine years in the United States House of Representatives and was elected Speaker in 1849. From 1851 through 1853 he was governor of Georgia, and during President James Buchanan's administration he was the secretary of the treasury (and the president's main advisor). In calmer times he might even have become president himself, and with his consummate skill in rough-and-tumble American politics he might also have made a better Confederate president than Jefferson Davis, a stiff, unbending West Pointer. Instead Cobb

had only limited success as a Confederate general. His younger brother Thomas R. R. Cobb (1839) was also a Confederate general, but earlier he had been a distinguished lawyer and legal scholar, one of the three founders of the law school at the University of Georgia in 1859, a potent secessionist politician and propagandist, and the main author of the Confederate constitution. A Yankee shell ended his brilliant career at the Battle of Fredericksburg late in 1862.

Eugenius A. Nisbet, top man in the senior class of three in 1821, served in the state and

This view of the campus appears as an engraving on the border of James R. Butts's very large and detailed map of Georgia published in 1859. From left to right are Phi Kappa Hall, Old College, New College, the Chapel, Demosthenian Hall, and a corner of the Ivy Building. The engraving also shows the sturdy oak tree in front of the Chapel where the expelled Robert Toombs is supposed to have held forth so elo-

quently that he drew out onto the lawn the commencement audience in the Chapel. Alas, the story is untrue— Toombs was thrown out in January 1828 and commencement was not until August! It seems to have originated as an anecdote in one of the famous speeches of Henry W. Grady (class of 1868). According to tradition, the tree was struck by lightning at the same time that Toombs died in 1885. Because of these stories (true or not), the tree and later the charred stump have always been known as the "Toombs

Oak." The wooden fence, designed to keep out the numerous dogs and occasional livestock that roamed the streets of Athens, was not replaced by the present iron fence and the famous Arch until the late 1850s.

national legislatures, became one of the original three justices of the state supreme court in 1845, and served with distinction for eight years. He ran unsuccessfully for the governorship twice. Though originally opposed to secession, at the state convention of 1861 he introduced the fateful resolution that carried Georgia out of the Union. Charles J. Jenkins had studied at Waddel's famous academy, but at Georgia he got into trouble and in 1822 Waddel sent

him away. After completing his education at Union College in New York, Jenkins, a moderate, became a power in the Georgia legislature. Immediately after the Civil War he served briefly as governor, and he chaired the state constitutional convention of 1877. He also served as president of the Board of Trustees of the university that had once expelled him.

Howell Cobb's colleague in the class of 1834,

> University of Geo.
> March 7th 1860
>
> Col D. C. Barrow,
> Athens,
> Dear Sir,
>
> I regret to be ordered by the Faculty to announce to you that yr son, Thos A. Barrow, is greatly neglecting his College duties and to say that he must make immediate and manifest improvement, in order to retain his rank in this Institution. With a view of effecting this we earnestly ask your co-operation. By order of the Faculty.
>
> With much respect,—
> Yr. mo. ob. Servt.—
> Wm Henry Waddell,
> Cor. Sec. Fac.

The antebellum faculty kept a close watch on the students and warned the parents when academic difficulties developed. William Henry Waddell, son of Moses Waddel and professor of ancient languages from 1858 to 1880, served as corresponding secretary of the faculty in 1860. Thomas Augustine Barrow was the son of a local planter and one of five brothers who graduated from the university. Apparently the letter served its purpose: Barrow received his A.B. in 1862. Thomas Barrow's younger brother David (class of 1874) became chancellor of the university in 1906.

Herschel V. Johnson, succeeded him as governor for the 1853–57 term. In 1860 Johnson ran as the vice-presidential candidate of Stephen A. Douglas and the Northern (not Southern) Democrats. He opposed secession, but when the war started he became a Confederate senator. Immediately after the war Georgia tried to send him and Aleck Stephens to the Senate, but the two former Confederate officials were not allowed to take their seats, and Johnson served as a state judge for the rest of his career.

Benjamin H. Hill, who came from a family that made great sacrifices to send him to the university, graduated with first honors in 1844 and became an outstanding lawyer. He served in the state legislature for a decade, and on one occasion turned aside Stephens's challenge to a duel with a joke. He opposed secession but then became a Confederate senator and strong supporter of President Davis. After the war he went to Washington, first as a congressman and then as a senator. Robert Toombs, sent away from the university in 1828, followed Jenkins to Union College. He served as a Whig congressman in the 1840s and as a senator in the 1850s, and after the election of Lincoln he championed secession passionately. He was the Confederacy's first secretary of state, but after five months he got bored and joined the army as a brigadier general. A good fighter but a poor strategist, he soon left the army in a row over promotion and spent most of the rest of the war holed up in Georgia, denouncing the Davis administration in Richmond and inadvertently damaging the Confederate war effort. He was

Joseph Henry Lumpkin entered the University of Georgia in *1812*, but the school seemed to be disintegrating, so he transferred to Princeton. After his graduation in *1819* he came home to Athens to practice law. He established the Phi Kappa Literary Society at Georgia in *1820*. When the Supreme Court of Georgia was established in *1845*, Lumpkin was appointed one of its three members and served as chief justice until *1867*. He became a champion of industrialization, and his judicial decisions paved the way for the commercial development of the New South after the Civil War. He was one of the founders of the University of Georgia School of Law and served as a trustee of the university.

supported in this states' rights opposition to President Davis by Governor Joseph E. Brown (a Yale man); by Aleck Stephens, the vice-president of the Confederacy, who spent most of his time in Georgia too; and by Stephens's brother Linton, who graduated with first honors from the University of Georgia in 1843 and became an influential state legislator. At the end of the war Toombs left for Europe just ahead of a detachment of Union cavalry. Returning in 1867, he remained one of Georgia's most thoroughly unreconstructed rebels. Toombs remained loyal to the University of Georgia, and he served on the Board of Trustees from 1859 until his death in 1885.

The university's elaborate commencement ceremonies in early August served as a meeting ground for virtually every active politician in the state. The Senatus Academicus remained a large, ungainly collection of state officeholders, but it did sometimes manage to gather a quorum at commencement time. The smaller, much more active, and equally politicized Board of Trustees always held its main meeting at this time. Even the smallest fish in Georgia politics found it advantageous to appear at commencement, and powerful outsiders like John C. Calhoun of neighboring South Carolina occasionally showed up to say a few words and join in the general politicking.

These graduation ceremonies lasted three to four days (and nights) and attracted flocks of people. Parents mingled with Athenians and country folks from the nearby counties, and a good number of slaves wangled a day off to join the festivities. The crowd heard long speeches by distinguished statesmen (politicians who kept getting re-elected), and each graduating senior also spoke—though his time was restricted to around ten minutes. The literary societies presented their more eloquent champions, and the crowd loved it all. Some preferred the dances and others liked the evening festivities, including a great deal of boisterous merrymaking after dark. Any graduate out three years or more could return and receive a master of arts degree for four dollars in cash, and many outsiders came to receive honorary degrees. Some well-to-do folk traveled long distances to see and be seen. In 1830 a northern visitor was astonished at the "fashion, taste, and refinement"

of Georgia's commencement, but he did not notice the wheeling and dealing that made Athens the political capital of the state for a few days in August. This kind of partisan politics flourished all over America, and it helped generate the tensions that finally led to civil war in 1861.

Although the university continued to produce outstanding graduates throughout the antebellum period, its future was never entirely secure. One of the most serious crises occurred during the 1850s, when the faculty clashed with President Church. Several problems led to the struggle, but at the bottom of the trouble lay the perennial shortage of funds. Financial support from the state increased slightly after the 1840s but remained minimal, and Church made no real effort to get more from the legislature. Student enrollment wavered at around one hundred and the faculty numbered seven or eight. The younger professors especially chafed and then began to resign; once in the 1850s the faculty briefly shrank to four men. The professors wanted to improve the University of Georgia, to change it from a restricted little college into a real university by broadening and modernizing its curriculum, putting more emphasis on scientific and other practical courses, and reducing the traditional stress on Greek and Latin. The faculty complained that comparable schools were beginning to pull ahead; more specifically, they were growing faster, they paid better salaries, they did not require as many housekeeping and policing duties of their faculty, and, above all, they were not run by Alonzo Church.

Church was not a villain; he had devoted his life to the university, but he had become set in his ways over the years. He served as professor of mathematics at the University of Georgia for forty years and as its president for thirty years. As the years went by he became more and more autocratic. Despite his deteriorating health he energetically fought off every faculty challenge, retaining the support of the Board of Trustees and its executive subcommittee, the Prudential Committee.

But on campus Church's popularity slipped steadily. The students became more critical of him; one described him as "surly as a restive

bull." An invitation to the president's home for dinner was considered a great coup, but mainly because at any given time at least half of the students fancied themselves in love with one of his beautiful daughters, Elvira, Sarah Jane, Lizzie, Julia, and Anna. In writing to a friend in 1835 one smitten student described Sarah Jane as "*Amiable, Pious, Accomplished, Talented & a great many think her handsome,*" and almost a decade later another student wrote in his diary that Lizzie was "certainly one of the most beautiful ladies in the world." But even his lovely daughters could not redeem Church's fading reputation, and the crisis of the 1850s steadily deepened.

The university faltered as one after another of its best professors resigned in anger and frustration. In 1853 the very able Charles F.

McCay became the fourth to leave when he accepted a better-paying position at South Carolina College. Two years later Carolina also got John LeConte, an outstanding teacher and scientist who became the sixth refugee from Georgia. By 1856 enrollment had slipped below one hundred for the first time in two decades, and the resultant loss of tuition increased the school's financial problems.

To ease the strain Church was forced to sell the school's botanical garden, which had been a source of great pride for the university and Athens. In 1849 William Gilmore Simms attended the university's commencement and penned his impressions for the Charleston newspapers under the pseudonym "The Wanderer." He wrote mainly about the "Botanic Garden"

Above: After graduating with first honors in the class of 1841, Thomas R. R. Cobb began a distinguished legal career in Athens. He codified the state's laws, and he also wrote on slave law. In 1858 he founded the Lucy Cobb Institute, an academy for young ladies in Athens. With Joseph Henry Lumpkin and William Hope Hull he established the University of Georgia School of Law, which initially operated in his and Lumpkin's law office, and he also served as a trustee of the university. A staunch secessionist, he helped lead Georgia out of the Union, and he was the main author of the Confederate constitution. He organized Cobb's Legion and went off to fight in Virginia; although Cobb had no military training, he performed competently. At the battle of Fredericksburg in December 1862 Cobb's men, dug in behind a stone wall, repulsed wave after wave of attacking Yankees, but at the height of this great Confederate victory Cobb was killed by Union artillery fire. Here he is shown as a young lawyer. (Courtesy of the University of Georgia School of Law.)

with its "handsome collection of flowers, flowering plants and shrubs, scattered over . . . several acres; in which is preserved a large portion of the original forest-trees, consisting of oaks, hickory, chesnut, maple and locust" and its "conservatory, or hot-house, glazed on top, and on three sides" containing many cactus plants and a lily pond in the center. Simms was impressed but noticed even then that "the condition of the garden wears somewhat the aspect of being neglected in culture, the hand of human labor being only here and there apparent."

Church hated to abandon the botanical garden, which had been his haven from the growing cares of his job. Partly to cushion the blow to the ailing "old man," the trustees provided that the one thousand dollars received for the garden would be used to replace the battered wooden fence along the front of the campus. A sturdy iron fence was manufactured at the Athens foundry and installed along with an elaborate gateway, the famous Arch, which remains the symbol of the university. Copied from the great seal of the state of Georgia, its three columns originally held a pair of iron gates which soon disappeared, leaving the Arch as it is today.

The day-to-day struggle with the faculty reached a climax in 1856, and Church submitted his resignation to the Board of Trustees. Reacting quickly, the board called for the resignation of the entire staff, the president and the faculty, and then promptly reinstated President Church and three of the less obstreperous faculty members. Joseph LeConte and two others were dismissed. LeConte joined his brother at South Carolina College, and the campus began to return to normal.

The trustees' strong support for Church cannot be construed as support for his conservative views. In fact, the board had already begun a thorough reorganization of the University of Georgia, aiming to change it from a small, traditional college into a modern university more attuned to the needs of the people of the state. By this time the antiquated, unwieldy Senatus Academicus was being abolished by the legislature, and the Board of Trustees emerged as the official as well as the real governing body. After much wrangling and revising, the trustees finally accepted a plan in 1859, just before Church retired. The university would be divided down the middle. The freshmen and sophomores would be moved northwestward almost two miles to a large new building designated the Collegiate Institute. There the younger students could be isolated and closely supervised until they were ready for the main campus. The juniors and seniors would form the college proper on the old campus. Much of the old curriculum would be retained, but advanced or specialized programs in medicine, law, agriculture, engineering, science, languages, and other fields would be added. Earned master of arts degrees and doctorates would be awarded, and the staff would be more than doubled to twenty professors.

This new, expanded university would be under the direction of a chancellor who would devote much of his time to traveling all over the state seeking private endowments and, more important, coaxing more state funds from the stingy legislature. His vice-chancellor or president would direct the day-to-day operation of the school. The enlarged faculty would be freed of most of the policing duties Church had insisted upon, and the students would be governed by a uniform system of demerits—nine of them meant automatic suspension.

It all looked fine on paper, but actual implementation of the program was another matter. Freshmen and sophomores reacted with bitter hostility to the idea of their banishment across town, so they stayed on the main campus, and the Collegiate Institute became University High School almost as soon as it was completed in 1862 (it was renamed Gilmer Hall when it became part of the State Normal School). The student body edged above a hundred again in 1860, and the staff increased to ten, including a few tutors. But the state never provided much more money, and the rest of the new program languished.

A law school did emerge in 1859, but only because it was independent of the university's regular budget. Thomas R. R. Cobb, Joseph Henry Lumpkin, and William Hope Hull (grandson of the Reverend Hope Hull and first honor graduate of the class of 1838) founded the University of Georgia School of Law, which accepted students with no college training for a two-session (one-year) course of study costing one hundred dollars in tuition and featuring lectures and practice court proceedings. Cobb and Hull taught regularly, and Lumpkin helped when the state supreme court was not in session. All classes were held in Cobb and Lumpkin's law office a few blocks from the campus, and the three teachers were paid from the school's tuition fees. This was the only immediate fruit of the university's new master plan, and though it barely survived its first decade, it eventually developed into the state's premier law school.

No one seemed to know where the money was coming from to bring forth the rest of the new, improved University of Georgia. Two distinguished (and worldly-wise) Georgians de-

Lucy Cobb Institute was established in 1859 as a preparatory school for young ladies. It flourished, becoming a popular place for the university's all-male student body to visit. During the depression of the 1930s the school closed. The building was transferred to the university, which used it as a women's dormitory, administrative offices, and a storage area. It now houses the Carl Vinson Institute of Government. During the 1960s the upper floor deteriorated so badly that it had to be removed. This photograph was taken in the 1860s.

clined the new chancellorship. Patrick H. Mell, a Baptist minister and a graduate of Amherst College who had been hired by Church in 1856 to teach ethics and metaphysics, accepted the vice-chancellorship, but only in 1860 did the trustees find a man brave and idealistic (and perhaps naive) enough to become the university's first chancellor.

Andrew A. Lipscomb, a native of Virginia, had received a solid basic education at local academies, but he entered the Methodist ministry at an early age and had never attended college. After many years of preaching he retired because of poor health, but soon he returned to work to champion the cause of advanced education for white women. Through the 1850s he directed first the Metropolitan Institute for Young Ladies and then the Tuskegee Female Institute in Alabama. When he assumed control of the University of Georgia, four decades of Presbyterian leadership ended, but the chancellorship would be filled by Protestant ministers until the turn of the century.

Almost as soon as Chancellor Lipscomb began his new work, he and his university were overwhelmed by the rush of outside events. Described as "a benevolent man, large-hearted and loving," he contrasted sharply with his stern Presbyterian predecessors, but beneath his gentle manner lay a toughness and determination that would soon be needed. On April 12, 1861, Confederate artillery opened fire on Fort Sumter in Charleston Harbor. The Civil War had begun, and the challenge of reorganizing the university soon yielded to the greater challenge of sheer survival.

41

Troubled Times,
1861–1899

The Confederate attack on Fort Sumter marked the beginning of a national tragedy. All over the nation men mobilized for combat. Even experienced military men could not envision the coming slaughter—the death of more than six hundred thousand Americans, northerners and southerners, out of a total population of thirty-one million. The nation's campuses fed the bloody battlefields with a steady stream of bright recruits, and nearly a hundred University of Georgia men gave their lives for the Confederacy.

Francis S. Bartow (class of 1835), a Savannah lawyer, urged secession at the state convention that carried Georgia out of the Union in January 1861. After a short time in the Confederate Congress, he led the first Georgia regiment to Virginia in May. Two months later he led five regiments at the First Battle of Bull Run and helped turn the tide for the Confederates, but his men were decimated and Bartow himself fell at the very moment of victory. Later the state gave his name to a county previously named for Lewis Cass (a famous Yankee politician).

Like Bartow, Henry Lewis Benning (first honor graduate of the class of 1834), did well in law and favored secession at the state convention of 1861. He too led a Georgia regiment into combat, but he survived the war with a splendid record. General Benning fought well through the whole war and was severely wounded at the Battle of the Wilderness in the spring of 1864, but he soon returned to the fighting and surrendered at Appomattox with Lee. "Old Rock" was a born soldier, and the United States Army later named its officer training school near his home in Columbus in his honor.

Even more famous was John B. Gordon, one of Lee's best generals. He studied at the University of Georgia for four years and impressed all with his junior oration at the commencement of 1852, but he went home to run a family business a few months before his own class graduated in 1853. Also a lawyer, Captain Gordon led a volunteer company to Virginia early in the war, and he rose rapidly in the Army of Northern Virginia through a series of bloody battles. A general at thirty-one, Gordon fought on to the end. After the war Gordon fashioned a whole new career in politics. In 1873 he was elected to the United States Senate, where he remained for seven years. After spending the next six years in railroading he became governor of Georgia in 1886, and in 1890 he returned to the Senate. He died in 1904. He remains one of Georgia's greatest heroes, and his equestrian statue on the grounds of the state capitol in Atlanta joins those of two other University of Georgia men: Eugene Talmadge (class of 1907) and Richard B. Russell, Jr. (1918).

One other former student played a major role in the Civil War, but he wore blue, not gray. Stephen Vincent Benet was a native of Florida, a descendant of early Spanish settlers. In 1845 he entered the junior class at Georgia but within the year transferred to West Point as the new state of Florida's first student there. After graduation Benet remained in the army, and in 1855 he accepted an honorary master of arts degree from the University of Georgia. When the Civil War began, Benet stayed in the Union army and helped direct the manufacture of weapons and ammunition behind the lines. After the war he became a brigadier general and chief of ordnance. The only recorded Union soldier from the university, General Benet was not exactly honored in Athens over the years, but time finally healed the old bitterness. In 1933, almost a century after young Benet's sojourn at the university, his grandson, a famous poet with the same name, came back on Alumni Day to present a portrait of the general in blue and to read an original poem honoring "the memory of those men who, on each side, fought for the thing they loved."

The prominent casualties are easily remembered, but the less famous Georgia students who vanished into the maelstrom are part of the same tragic story. Benjamin Mell was the top man among the twenty-two seniors in 1861. His father, the vice-chancellor, organized a troop at once but was too old for active service. Benjamin joined his father's unit and went straight to the front. A fine fighting soldier, he wrote his father in the spring of 1862 from the killing grounds east of Richmond, describing a wounded comrade: "The poor fellow was lying on a platform under a tree in the edge of a field. I saw the leg cut off and thrown aside. . . . I believe I had rather be shot dead than mutilated in that way." He died courageously that fall at the Battle of Crampton's Gap. Six more of Mell's class were killed in battle.

William G. Delony graduated first in the class of 1846. A few years later he served briefly as a tutor in ancient languages at the university, but soon he was concentrating on the practice of law in and around Athens. Happily married with a growing family, recently elected to the state legislature, Delony was just beginning to enjoy success when the war erupted. He organized a cavalry troop and rode off to Virginia. He led his men in fifty fights or skirmishes, received several serious wounds, and rose steadily to the rank of colonel. Delony's steady stream of letters home to his wife Rosa mentioned over and over his eagerness to be with his family in Athens again. But he was a soldier, hardened by two years of combat, and in a letter to Rosa dated September 5, 1863, he wrote candidly: "Strange as it may appear to one at home, there is a fascination in danger which allures a soldier, and perhaps it is well that it is so to those who are soldiers from necessity and a sense of duty. It serves to render tolerable many of the discomforts and burdens of our life." Eighteen days later Delony was badly wounded in the leg in a skirmish. He was taken to a hospital in Washington as a prisoner and died there early in October.

In Athens Chancellor Lipscomb and President Mell struggled to keep the University of Georgia going despite the war. Over half the students left when the war started, and the remaining enrollment of fifty or so steadily dwindled as the war continued. Even the few who were not eager to fight (or whose parents would not let them go) gradually were called up temporarily with the militia or drafted permanently. Finally, in September 1863, the university suspended operations. Thereafter it housed mainly refugees but also wounded Confederate soldiers and, briefly, Yankee prisoners of war. Most other southern colleges went through the same gradual decline during the war, and in Georgia only Wesleyan College for women flourished as the Confederacy slowly crumbled under the relentless assault of Union armies.

Finally, in the spring of 1865, the war ended. Lee surrendered in Virginia, and what was left of the Confederate armies disbanded and came home. A terrible blight settled over the whole South as the hated Yankees came to begin Reconstruction. The University of Georgia was part of this defeated, disspirited South. The bold plan of 1859 for expansion and reform seemed hopeless; the question now was whether the university could survive. Chancellor Lipscomb had kept the school open as long as possible during the war, and as soon as the war ended he set to work to reopen it.

The university held classes in January 1866 with nearly eighty students, and the following year enrollment rose to 265, though almost a hundred of those students attended University High School off the main campus. Most of the new men were veterans of the Confederate army, and they were a tough, proud lot. Many had been wounded, a few showed empty sleeves as badges of combat, and one cocky fellow insisted on wearing his outlawed Rebel uniform for the sophomore class photograph in 1866. Even those who had been too young for the war

All twenty-two seniors in the class of 1861 went to war; seven never returned. Among the fallen was Benjamin Mell (left), top man in the class and son of Professor Patrick H. Mell, who later became chancellor. Young Mell, a fine soldier, quickly made sergeant. Tough and confident, he marched with Lee's army as it swept into Maryland in the fall of 1862, and he was cut down by rifle fire in the Battle of Crampton's Gap. All told, nearly a hundred Georgia men died for the South.

Facing page: Henry L. Benning, the son of a prosperous planter, graduated first in the class of 1834. He opened a law practice in Columbus and became a wealthy planter as well. When the Civil War began he became colonel of a Confederate infantry regiment. A natural warrior, he led his brigade brilliantly, and by 1863 he was a brigadier general. He fought in many major battles and received one severe wound, but he survived the war and practiced law again until his death in 1875. The United States Army recognized Benning's military ability by naming its officer-training facilities near Columbus in his honor. This portrait of Benning is by Bjorn Eagele.

seemed more mature; Chancellor Lipscomb called them "a new race of students . . . more manly . . . more obedient . . . more thoughtful and prudent."

Federal troops had briefly occupied all but one of the university's buildings. Athenians resented their presence, but in truth their highjinks and vandalism were little worse than the antics of antebellum students. Radical Reconstruction in 1867 caused more bitterness. Former slaves now wandered freely around Athens, but when some attempted to enter university buildings, they were driven away by armed students.

The campus remained tense, and in August when commencement was held for the five graduating seniors, trouble erupted. Everything went smoothly until the junior orator, Albert Cox (a Confederate veteran), spoke on "The Vital Principle of Nations." Taking little more than ten minutes, he called on the South to "show a brave heart, determined will and quickened intellect" in the struggle for justice and truth, and he threw in some passionate verbiage like "here where gleams a bayonet hostile to our every interest" and "fling out in bold defiance the unconquered banner of your principles." At

47

The class of 1868 posing during their sophomore year, 1866. Almost all were veterans of the Confederate army. These students were far more mature than their antebellum counterparts, and the class of 1868 produced many outstanding Georgians. Henry W.

Grady (in the hat on the left between the last two rows) was too young for the war, but his father had fallen at Petersburg. On the back row, fourth from the right, George Bancroft appears to be wearing a Confederate uniform, which was strictly forbidden by occupation authorities. On the front row sits the

entire faculty: William L. Jones, James P. Waddell (the son of Moses Waddel), Patrick Mell (chancellor from 1878 to 1888), Andrew A. Lipscomb (chancellor from 1860 to 1874), Williams Rutherford, Louis Jones, and Leon Henri Charbonnier.

the end of his dramatic speech a band struck up "Dixie," and the audience whooped and hollered well into the evening, leaving the handful of Yankee soliders present more than a little chagrined.

Word soon reached General John Pope in Atlanta, and he immediately cut off all state funds to the university and ordered it closed. Only quick action and fast talk by Chancellor Lipscomb in Atlanta and Trustee Ben Hill in Washington salvaged the situation. The university reopened in September on schedule with 180 students on campus and another 90 at University High School, but the faculty returned to the old custom of censoring controversial poli-

tics out of the students' commencement speeches.

By the next year, 1868, the senior class had grown to thirty-eight (accompanied by nine graduates in law), and it was one of the most distinguished in the school's history. Albert Cox, who delivered a proper, tame oration at this commencement, became a prominent lawyer in Atlanta and a state legislator. Henry W. Grady became one of the nation's most famous journalists, and virtually all of their serious, mature classmates did well in business and the professions.

Slowly the University of Georgia recovered and moved ahead, but, even more than usual, money was a problem. The Civil War had shat-

The Library Building was the last addition in President Alonzo Church's grand plan for the antebellum campus, but he had retired by the time it was completed in 1862. The iron fence and the Arch appeared just be- *fore his retirement. The school's limited collection of books was housed on the second floor, the first floor included a hall that held three hundred people, and the top floor housed the university's museum collections. In 1905 the Library Building and the* *Ivy Building were joined by a classical façade to make the Academic Building. This photograph, taken around 1875, appeared in* Davis's Souvenir Album.

tered the southern economy, and the school's meager financial reserves had been invested in Confederate bonds, now worthless. After some delays, the state's annual contribution of eight thousand dollars resumed, but that had been inadequate even before the war. Doubling the tuition to one hundred dollars a year helped somewhat, and, more important, in 1866 the legislators passed a law granting injured, poor veterans three hundred dollars a year to attend one of the major colleges in Georgia, in return requiring them to teach in the state for as many years as they received this aid. Many veterans took advantage of the state's help and enrolled at the University of Georgia. Their tuition pay-

ments greatly aided the school, which assigned most of these poorly prepared newcomers to the University High School across town. Still, the university remained near bankruptcy.

Finally the federal government came to the rescue. While the South had been trying to fight its way out of the Union, Congress passed the Morrill Land Grant College Act of 1862, which provided financial support for "such branches of learning as are related to agriculture and the mechanic arts." As soon as the war ended the former Confederate states were allowed to get their share of public lands, which in 1866 translated into $243,000 for Georgia. For five years nothing was done with this bonanza, but just before time ran out, the state turned the funds over to the University of Georgia, which by state law had to invest them to generate an annual income of around $16,000.

Thus in 1872 the Georgia State College of Agriculture and the Mechanic Arts was established at the university in Athens. Technically it was a separate school, and, unlike the old university, it charged no tuition and required no entrance examination. Yet in reality the two schools were one, with the same faculty, the same facilities, and the same Board of Trustees. Even the president of the new school, William Leroy Broun, had long been a professor of natural philosophy (science) at the university.

The sponsors of the Morrill Act had not envisioned such a close, almost parasitic relationship, which allowed the old university to soak up the interest on the original federal funds while maintaining almost total dominance over the A&M College. But this arrangement probably saved the university during the long, hard decades after the Civil War. By 1873 Georgia had over three hundred students; more than half of them were enrolled in the A&M College, which was crowded into Philosophical Hall. Certainly the new arrangement reinvigorated the university and allowed it to try to continue the reforms and expansion started in 1859.

Chancellor Lipscomb began to change the university even before the A&M College opened. A champion of the midwestern concept of large diversified state universities committed to public service, he diluted the old classical curriculum and added many practical courses. He favored the lecture system in class and introduced many elective courses for juniors and seniors. Josiah Meigs would probably have approved, but Chancellor Lipscomb was ahead of his time in conservative Georgia. The legislature withheld the funds necessary to make most of his reforms work, but the seed was planted, and at the turn of the century it would burst forth in full flower, tirelessly cultivated by two of Lipscomb's students, Walter B. Hill (class of 1870) and David C. Barrow (class of 1874).

Meanwhile, because most Confederate veterans had completed their studies, University High School across town closed. The opening of the A&M College the same year took up some of the slack, and the high school building, Rock College, became the headquarters for the new model farm.

The university also began to expand into other areas of the state. North Georgia Agricultural College at Dahlonega became a department of the university in 1873. This two-year school, which had just opened in the old United States Mint Building, became the first of a series of branch colleges designed to channel students to the main campus in Athens for further work. This feeder system never functioned properly, however, and the new satellite institutions gradually either faded away or evolved into fully independent colleges. The absorption of the Medical College of Georgia in 1874 added another department to the university, but the medical school, so promising in the antebellum period, had come upon hard times and had to struggle just to survive.

On the main campus in Athens Lipscomb made a few more changes. He tried to convert the austere dormitories in Old College and New College into more pleasant "students' homes" by bringing a local family into each to add a touch of traditional domesticity. Also, much to the joy of the students, he reduced the number of required chapel services.

Facing page: A section of a map of Athens and the university drawn in 1874 by W. W. Thomas. Athens was developing into a busy town, and in 1871 it became the county seat of Clarke County. At the same time the university's enrollment was actually declining from a high of 312 in 1873 toward a low of 116 in 1878. The only sign of progress was Moore College, built in 1874 to house the State College of Agriculture and the Mechanic Arts (A&M College). Otherwise the campus seemed unchanged: the Library Building, Museum (the Ivy Building), the literary society buildings, the Chapel, State College (Moore College), New College, Old College, Laboratory (Philosophical Hall), and five faculty houses. The campus ended at Baldwin Street, and beyond Tanyard Branch lay a wooded area labeled as the estate of Governor Wilson Lumpkin. The old Rock House, which would remain standing in the shadow of Conner Hall, is not even shown on the future south campus of the university. The Athens Manufacturing Company just southeast of the old campus was better known to students during the mid-1970s through the mid-1990s as O'Malley's, a popular gathering place. (Courtesy of the Athens Historical Society.)

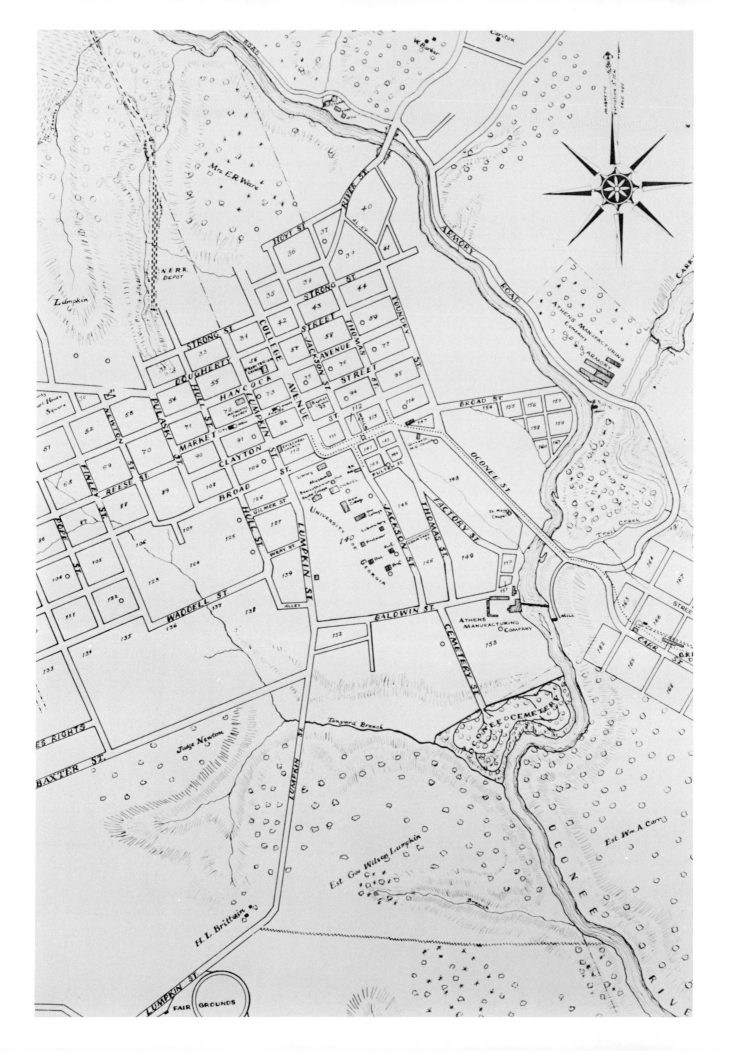

Other significant campus changes developed unofficially. Baseball began to emerge as a popular sport not long after the Civil War. Teams popped up in fields and cow pastures all over town and campus, and some teams traveled to find new opponents. One campus team went all the way to Augusta to pound out a 61 to 21 victory. The antebellum policy of sponsoring no organized sports disappeared only slowly; not until the early 1890s did the university plunge into the turbulent world of intercollegiate athletics.

Just as significant was the coming of the Greeks. Jabez L. M. Curry, a Georgia alumnus who became president of Howard College, recalled some sort of secret organizations on campus back in his student days in the 1840s, but national or regional Greek-letter fraternities came right after the Civil War. Sigma Alpha Epsilon appeared in 1866, and right behind came Chi Phi, Kappa Alpha, and Phi Delta Theta. By the 1880s eight fraternities flourished. The old Phi Kappa and Demosthenian literary societies began to fade as athletics and social fraternities reshaped social life on the campus.

Larger national trends had even greater impact. The Panic of 1873 ushered in a long, grinding depression that especially ravaged the already-battered South. In 1874 Lipscomb, wearying of the struggle for reform and worrying about his health, retired (and lived on until 1890). Enrollment at the university slipped below 270 in these hard times, and the Board of Trustees had difficulty finding someone to accept the chancellorship.

Finally, Henry H. Tucker, a Baptist minister who had been president of Mercer for six years, accepted the honor—and the challenge. The first native Georgian to lead the university, the conservative Tucker whittled away at Lipscomb's reforms, soon eliminating the new elective courses. In 1878 a special committee of trustees chaired by Aleck Stephens formally shaped a new curriculum. The university proper would grant three degrees: the traditional A.B., stressing Latin and Greek; a B.S., requiring only one classical language; and a new bachelor of philosophy degree, requiring no classical language at all. The A&M College

would offer degrees in agriculture, engineering, and chemistry. The student could elect his degree program, but then he faced a fixed curriculum with no electives. The law school would continue to offer a one-year course with no entrance requirements, and soon a little graduate work developed, mainly in civil and mining engineering.

Tucker succeeded in dismantling many of Lipscomb's reforms, but he was not a popular chancellor. Like old Josiah Meigs, he was outspoken and abrasive. Consequently, he often failed, as when he tried to destroy the new fraternities but only succeeded in driving them underground temporarily. He did do yeoman service in fighting off the mounting attacks on the University of Georgia by the Baptists and Methodists. A Baptist himself, he counterattacked effectively. Still, enrollment at the university continued to erode. The loss of students was due to the relentless depression, but Chancellor Tucker, the man in charge, was held responsible. Oglethorpe College had already collapsed and would not open again until the twentieth century. Mercer moved to Macon and Emory to Atlanta as they too struggled to survive through the hard times.

The legislature continued its anemic support of the university, and the only major new building, Moore College (1874), was constructed not with state money but with twenty-five thousand dollars contributed entirely by the people of Athens. This late French Renaissance structure behind the Library Building and facing Broad Street became the new home of the A&M College, and Philosophical Hall was leased to Irene Ruff, a war widow who ran a boarding house for students there. Moore College was designed by Professor Leon Henri Charbonnier, who had graduated from St. Cyr, the West Point of France, and then served as a captain in the French army in north Africa until poor health forced his retirement. He came to the University of Georgia at the beginning of the Civil War and taught at the University High School, where he also drilled the students in military tactics. After the war he taught mathematics, physics, astronomy, and civil engineering at the university, and after 1872 he also directed the military training required at all land-grant colleges. Most students enjoyed drilling under

In 1883 David Crenshaw Barrow was made professor of engineering and in 1889 professor of mathematics and engineering. One of the high

points of the civil engineering program was a week-long field trip in the spring when the class camped out and surveyed a rail line through the countryside near Athens. This photograph

shows a class with the tools they took on their field trip. Barrow is standing in the center. (Courtesy of Susan B. Tate.)

"Colonel Charby," especially since they got to wear Confederate gray uniforms and were excused when they became seniors. By the time he finally retired in 1898, the wiry little Frenchman had become a leading figure on campus.

Chancellor Tucker, on the other hand, lasted only until 1878, when he was eased out by the trustees and replaced by Patrick H. Mell. Like Tucker a native Georgian and a Baptist clergyman, Mell had come to the university in 1857 and had served as vice-chancellor for many years. During Mell's decade as chancellor condi-

tions at the university did not noticeably improve, primarily because the state's economy was depressed. By 1880 Georgia had over a million and a half citizens, 817,000 whites and 725,000 blacks. Many had fallen into some form of the stifling sharecropping system, and industrial development was still very limited. The segregated public school system offered the masses at best a few years of primary education; high school remained the exception rather than the rule for whites and especially for blacks.

Chancellor Mell himself was partly responsible for the university's difficulties. Like most of

53

his predecessors, he was not aggressive in seeking greater support for the university. Enrollment hovered around two hundred. The A&M College suffered the greatest loss; it had fewer students than the Dahlonega branch, even though it had no entrance requirements. All too often enthusiastic youngsters from farms found themselves unable to handle advanced academic work. Some dropped out quickly, but others stayed to struggle through basic remedial courses. Either way they went back home with no real agricultural expertise. Disappointed and angered, the farmers themselves began to turn against the university, increasingly convinced that it remained what it had always been to them, a small, isolated, rich boys' school with no concern for the rural masses.

Not surprisingly, the state continued to give only limited support to the university. The federal government through the land-grant college system continued to furnish the vast majority of operating funds, and the university continued to channel almost all of these funds into traditional operations, leaving the A&M College practically a phantom institution. Even funds that actually reached the college increasingly drained away to Dahlonega and new branch colleges at Cuthbert, Thomasville, Milledgeville, and Hamilton and to the new Agricultural Experiment Station at Griffin (which Mell tried but failed to locate in Athens).

These new branches within the university system caused only minor difficulties in comparison with a major new branch that would come to rival the parent university in Athens. The New South emphasis on industrial and urban growth inevitably led to the demand for a modern school of technology, and in 1885 the legislature appropriated the huge sum of sixty-five thousand dollars. Then the fight began over the location of the new college. Even Emory briefly flirted with the idea of technical education, and Chancellor Mell championed his university, which, after all, already had a good number of courses in science and a department of civil engineering.

By this time Athens had developed some light industry and considerable commercial activity. With almost ten thousand inhabitants, it had become more than just a college town. Since 1875 the seat of Clarke County (the state's smallest),

it had independently raised the funds for Moore College early in the 1870s, but now it found itself competing with the city of Atlanta. The state capital since 1868, Atlanta already had a population of forty thousand and was on the verge of a period of explosive growth. Moving aggressively, it made an offer the state could not refuse: nine acres of land for a campus, seventy thousand dollars at once and twenty-five hundred annually. Even Henry W. Grady of the *Constitution,* a graduate and a trustee of the university, trumpeted the Atlanta location. Athens gave up the struggle, and in 1888 the Georgia Institute of Technology opened, offering a bachelor's degree in mechanical engineering.

Technically only another branch of the university in Athens, Tech operated with almost complete independence from the start and soon emerged as a significant school in its own right. The two schools developed a heated and sometimes bitter rivalry, which the coming of intercollegiate athletics in the 1890s magnified.

Shaken by the losing battles to keep the technical school and agricultural experiment station in Athens, elderly Chancellor Mell died in January 1888. Colonel Charbonnier, the vice-chancellor, ran the university until the Reverend William E. Boggs took over as the new chancellor the next year.

A native of India (the son of Presbyterian missionaries), Boggs graduated from South Carolina College, became a Presbyterian minister, served as a Confederate chaplain, and ministered to many congregations before coming to Athens at the age of fifty-one. At a time when many state universities had started broadening their curricula and emphasizing research and public service, Boggs continued the conservative policies of his predecessors, Tucker and Mell. Even as the state's population climbed toward two million, enrollment at the University of Georgia continued to fluctuate around two hundred, though it did edge up to about three hundred by the end of the century. The university continued to serve an infinitesimally small percentage of the people of the state.

The faculty grew only a little, to sixteen or eighteen professors and a few tutors in the 1890s, but a group of new professors changed

Because the campus dormitories were somewhat battered and very noisy, serious students often retreated to quieter boardinghouses off campus. Here Hugh M. Dorsey of Fayetteville (a Kappa Alpha) studies while his roommate, Telamon Cuyler Smith, takes a photograph. After receiving his A.B. in 1893, Dorsey studied law at the University of Virginia and then practiced in Atlanta. In 1913 he gained nationwide attention as the successful prosecutor of Leo M. Frank in the dramatic Mary Phagan murder case. His political career blossomed, and he served two terms as governor (1917–21) before resuming his law practice in Atlanta and finally serving as judge of the city court. He died in 1948.

the academic environment considerably. The Virginia-Maryland area became a fertile field for recruiting, supplanting the original Yale connection. In 1886 Charles M. Snelling, a graduate of the Virginia Military Institute, came to teach mathematics and relieve Charbonnier of the chore of drilling the cadets. Hampden-Sydney, Waddel's alma mater, furnished two professors who served the university for over half a century: Willis Henry Bocock came in 1889 and taught ancient languages (mainly Greek), and William Davis Hooper arrived a year later as a specialist in Latin. A year after that John H. T. McPherson came with the new Ph.D. degree from Johns Hopkins, one of the first American universities to copy the highly specialized German system of advanced education. McPherson organized the history department at the university and taught that subject for more than fifty years. Henry Clay White from the University of Virginia headed the chemistry department for fifty-five years. For a time he also served as president of the phantom A&M College. John and Sylvanus Morris grew

up on the campus as faculty children. John graduated from Randolph-Macon College in Virginia and did advanced work at the University of Berlin before returning to Athens to teach German for fifty-two years. Sylvanus received M.A. and law degrees from the University of Georgia, practiced law in Athens, joined the law school in 1895 and served as its dean from 1900 to 1929. Joseph Lustrat, educated at the Sorbonne in Paris, came to the university in 1897, just as Professor Charbonnier was retiring after thirty-seven years of service. Thus the connection with France continued unbroken as Lustrat served as head of the Romance language department for thirty years.

This new generation of professors generally had more formal training than their predecessors, but they too served primarily as teachers and generalists. Charles Holmes Herty was an exception. A native of Milledgeville, he received his Ph.B. degree from Georgia in 1886 and went on to Johns Hopkins to earn a Ph.D. in chemistry. He returned to the University of

Facing page: By 1893 Old College (often called Yahoo Hall) had deteriorated badly, but hardy students were allowed to room there rent free. Here the proud few come out on the steps in the springtime to pose lightheartedly for a not-very-formal photograph. The photographer, Telamon Cuyler, later wrote a description of the building on the back of the photograph: "The heating was by open-fires; lighting lamps

& candles. No running water etc: a dismal old rookery when I knew it—occupied by the poorest (or most penurious) students, who took their meals in boarding houses scattered about town. The caps and uniforms are of Student Cadet Corps: other costumes are of the period."

Above: Baseball became popular after the Civil War, and many town and campus teams were formed. This game is being played in 1893 on the rough athletic field back of New College. The catcher is well padded, and the tense batter is Samuel H. Sibley of Union Point, who received his A.B. in 1892 and his LL.B. in 1893. He was a federal district judge for twelve years and served for seventeen years on the United States Circuit Court of Appeals for the Deep South. Photograph by Telamon Cuyler.

Though the 1896 Pandora *listed this group as the varsity boat crew, the shot put and cleated shoes indicate track activities. This photograph was made at the McDannell Studio in Athens, which provided the painted backdrop.*

Georgia and taught chemistry from 1891 to 1899, but in order to win promotion he moved on to the University of North Carolina, where he taught for many years. Herty spent even more of his time as a research chemist outside of academia. His discoveries gained him an international reputation, and in the South his contributions to the commercial pine industry were particularly valuable.

Like many others frustrated at the University of Georgia, Herty remained a loyal alumnus, and in his one decade of teaching there he made one crucial contribution: almost single-handed he organized intercollegiate athletics at

the university. Herty had been an avid sportsman while a student at the university in the middle 1880s, and he had heartily desired a more organized athletic program. Baseball was the only active team sport. Each class had a team—Herty was a substitute on the senior squad of 1886—and pick-up games flourished. Very crude, disorganized kickball or football games were played between students on the rough field west of New College. A few students lifted weights or ran a little or played at tennis, and a few had boxing gloves, though the traditional fist fights were much more common

Alpha Tau Omega, 1899. This typical fraternity photograph includes on the top row, fourth from the left, Ulrich Bonnell Phillips (A.B. 1897) who was one of the university's few graduate students. Studying history under John H. T. McPherson, he also served as a tutor (today's graduate teaching assistant) until 1899, when he received his M.A. Then he moved on to Columbia University, where, after being rebuffed in his effort to return to Georgia as chief librarian, he received a Ph.D. in 1902. He concluded a brilliant career as a teaching and writing scholar at Yale University. Phillips gained recognition as one of the nation's most distinguished historians before his death in 1934. The first of his many publications appeared as an article in the 1899 Pandora *that described the University of Georgia's early struggles, lamented its long stagnation after the Civil War, and called on "the coming generation to wipe this stain from Georgia's scutcheon." (Photograph from the 1899* Pandora.)

than formal boxing matches. The cadets drilled more or less regularly, and a small rifle team evolved. By 1894 three boats with crews of four somehow raced on the Oconee River.

Every spring the whole school turned out for Field Day, a kind of intramural track meet. By 1890 this was organized well enough to record officially the triumphs of William W. Gordon, Jr., who swept the fifty-yard dash ($5\frac{4}{5}$ seconds), the hundred ($10\frac{3}{5}$ seconds), and the high jump (five feet, two inches). John R. Cooper won the shot put (thirty-six feet, six inches) and the heavyweight wrestling, and for good measure caught the greased pig. After finishing at Georgia Gordon studied law at Harvard and Columbia. He served as a volunteer officer in the war against Spain in 1898 and then practiced law

Forming in front of the Library Building (now the north side of the Academic Building), the officers of the cadet corps stand inspection in their dress uniforms. In the background to the right is Phi Kappa Hall. Barely visible to the left of the white screen are the school's earliest real tennis courts. This photograph was taken near the turn of the century by William Munroe White. (Courtesy of William E. White.)

successfully in Savannah. His friend Cooper received a law degree from Georgia and established a lucrative practice in Macon.

Athletics became much more serious when Herty returned to the campus the next year. The students had chosen red and black as the school colors; they had decided to drop yellow because of its suggestion of cowardice. The first mascot, a goat, was soon abandoned as the monopoly of the nearby Lucy Cobb Institute, a finishing school for young women, and a female bull terrier named Trilby reigned in the 1890s.

On January 30, 1892, Herty brought the first official football game to Athens. The game was played on the rough field behind New College, and Mercer fell by a score of 50 to 0. Three weeks later in Atlanta, Georgia lost to Auburn by a score of 10 to 0. The following year Georgia Tech came to Athens and won a bitter, riotous battle by a score of 28 to 6. Eligibility requirements were vague in those days. The star of Tech's victory was a former Harvard athlete and future United States Army general named Leonard Wood, then an army captain stationed at Fort McPherson, and some of the students at the University of Georgia School of Law (which had no entrance requirements) played for the red and black over the years. More significantly, the rules were too loose and the protective equipment was inadequate. When a game against Virginia in Atlanta in 1897 ended in the death of a Georgia player, Von Gammon, a drive to abolish the sport developed. All over the nation football was causing many serious injuries and some deaths. A bill abolishing football sailed through the state legislature, but

60

Social fraternities grew very rapidly on the campus after the Civil War, but a good number of students did not join them. Many belonged instead to the

Non-Fraternity Club, which took its place in the Pandora *along with other campus organizations. Here some of*

the forty-nine "Nons" of 1899 pose for their own group portrait by William Munroe White. (Courtesy of William E. White.)

Herty continued to champion the game, insisting that better facilities and equipment would eliminate excessive dangers, and Von Gammon's mother defended Herty and football, the game her son "held so dear." Governor William Y. Atkinson had graduated in law from the university in 1877 and had been a trustee since 1891. A sports enthusiast, he had witnessed the fatal game in Atlanta. After much thought, he refused to sign the bill, and football survived in Georgia.

A few years earlier the legislature had intervened to make another significant change at the university. The elitist, self-perpetuating Board of Trustees, which had grown to forty-one members, had become almost as unwieldy as

the long-defunct Senatus Academicus had been, so it was abolished in 1889, and a new board was set up in its place. The governor of Georgia, John B. Gordon (class of 1853), appointed the first members; one trustee came from each congressional district, two from Athens (a relic of the old Prudential Committee), and four from the state at large. The governor and three other ex-officio members completed the new, streamlined board, which would be more responsive to popular pressures.

A few years later, in 1896, the legislature appropriated funds ($22,600) for a major new building on campus for the first time since the Civil War. By 1897 a large brick building with cupola was completed just south of Phi Kappa Hall. At first it housed the English and modern language departments on the first floor, the ancient languages department on the second floor, and the biology department on the top floor. At the turn of the century it was named Science Hall, an indication of new directions at the university.

But the legislature also served as a forum for some fierce attacks on the university. The denominational colleges continued to criticize the University of Georgia, especially after 1881, when it abolished all tuition payments. In 1889 President Warren A. Candler of Emory denounced "Calvinists" (Presbyterians) like Chancellor Boggs as well as the whole concept of higher education in public institutions. Rebuttals were presented to the legislators by the chairman of the Board of Trustees, N. J. Hammond (class of 1870), and William H. Felton (class of 1842), a trustee and a legislator. Felton's wife, Rebecca, also spoke out for the university, while chiding it for still refusing to admit females—the only woman on the staff was Sarah A. Frierson, the amateur librarian. The legislature took no action, but the denominational colleges continued to accuse the university of godlessness and debauchery.

At the same time James B. Hunnicutt, the university's only professor of agriculture, publicly denounced the university's neglect of agricultural education. The justice of Hunnicutt's criticism became plain in 1892, when the university abandoned its experimental farm at the former University High School across town. Rock College, renamed Gilmer Hall, became the first building of the new State Normal School, which, though technically another branch of the university, actually operated on its own. Strongly supported by the citizens of Athens, it progressed rapidly, and in the 1930s it became the Coordinate Campus of the university for female students and finally in the 1950s the United States Navy Supply Corps School.

Under the pressure of legislative investigations of why federal land-grant funds (as much as 70 percent of the university's annual appropriations) so seldom actually reached the A&M College, Chancellor Boggs shifted a few more

resources to the university's agricultural operations and even initiated occasional agricultural extension institutes around the state, but the University of Georgia remained isolated and remote from the people as it quietly tried to abandon some of its branch schools, which had always operated rather independently anyway. Chancellor Boggs's prestige had eroded, and in 1899 he resigned. As the century ended the University of Georgia seemed increasingly obsolescent; it looked more and more like an antebellum institution trying to live beyond its time.

A little modernization had occurred, and small signs of new life popped up sporadically to offer a little hope. Georgia's Civil War governor, Joseph E. Brown, a Yale man whose sons attended the university after the war, gave generously to the university, and so did Charles F. McCay, one of the faculty members who had resigned during President Church's tenure. In 1886 the Greek fraternities cooperated to bring forth the *Pandora*, one of the early yearbooks of the South, and they continued to control it for many years. The *Georgia University Magazine*, founded in 1851, was revived in the 1870s and was published off and on until the mid-1890s, when it was replaced by the *Georgian*. A new campus publication, the *Georgia Collegian*, appeared in 1870 but lasted only a few years. It was succeeded in 1884 by the *University Reporter*, a weekly paper that Chancellor Boggs suppressed in 1891 after it published some articles critical of the faculty. In 1893 the *Red and Black* stepped into the breach. Like the *Reporter* it was edited by the two literary societies, but after a brief suppression it was taken over by the Athletic Association in 1896. The *Red and Black* continued its rather erratic career into the twentieth century. The university's daily journal for many years, it became a completely independent newspaper in 1980. By the 1890s an underground newspaper called the *Bumble Bee* ("I sting where I light and I light often") appeared occasionally with some fairly sharp attacks on a few of the faculty. It too survived into the twentieth century, but eventually it faded away.

The Thalians brought dramatics to the campus in 1893 and the Blackfriars soon followed, but for many years the only respectable settings for performances were in town and, by the

Physics classes were held in Moore College until after the Second World War. In this photograph, taken about 1899, three undergraduates work with an in-

duction coil apparatus that feeds high voltage into the electrodes of the gaseous discharge globe to create ionization within the globe (in front of the middle student). To the right rests a

Wimshurst electrostatic generator, ready for use. Photograph by William Munroe White. (Courtesy of William E. White.)

1930s, at the Seney-Stovall Chapel at Lucy Cobb Institute. The YMCA appeared on campus, along with many less serious clubs (the Irish Club, the Alabama Club), most of which lasted only a few years. A major landscaping effort in 1881 added four hundred trees to the bare campus, but many buildings remained dilapidated. At heart the university was still a liberal-arts college much like Mercer and Emory and other small schools from the past.

As in the antebellum period, the University of Georgia continued to produce many graduates who succeeded in business and the professions, and a very high percentage of the leading poli-

ticians in the state continued to come from the university, especially the law school. Clark Howell (class of 1883) had a long career in the legislature and ran unsuccessfully for the governorship in 1906, but he is best remembered as Grady's successor at the *Atlanta Constitution*. Richard B. Russell, Sr. (class of 1879) also ran unsuccessfully for the governorship but then served for many years as chief justice of the state supreme court. He was a member of the Board of Trustees and sent his son and namesake to the university; the younger Russell became governor in 1931 and served thirty-eight consecutive years in the United States Senate, where he became one of the most powerful

The campus around 1899 with, from left to right, Old College, New College, the Chapel with its bell tower, *Demosthenian Hall, and the Ivy Building with a few students on the* *front steps. In the foreground the old iron fence runs along the walk beside Broad Street.*

men in the nation. Mercer men occasionally took the governorship in the 1890s, but as the twentieth century matured Georgia alumni acquired a near monopoly on the office.

A few other Georgia graduates attracted wide attention in their specialties. Eugene Robert Black received his A.B. in 1892, married the daughter of Henry W. Grady, and practiced law for many years in Atlanta. He eventually went into banking, became a governor of the Federal Reserve Bank of Atlanta, and in 1933 went to Washington to serve on the Board of Governors of the entire Federal Reserve System. Samuel H. Sibley, a fine baseball player, also received his A.B. in 1892 and stayed on to earn a law

degree the next year. He served with distinction for twelve years as a federal district judge and then moved up to serve ably for another seventeen years on the United States Circuit Court of Appeals for the Deep South. Another good baseball player who made it all the way to the United States Supreme Court, Joseph Rucker Lamar, attended Georgia from 1873 to 1875.

Ulrich Bonnell Phillips, a native of La Grange, received his A.B. degree in 1897 and remained in academic life. One of the university's first modern graduate students, he served as a tutor. He also worked to improve the growing library, and he supervised it in the evening.

After he received his A.M. in history in 1899, he entered Columbia University, where he received his Ph.D. in 1902. He taught at the University of Wisconsin and the University of Michigan and concluded his career at Yale, marking the first time talent had flowed northward in the old Georgia–Yale connection. Phillips's books on antebellum Georgia and the South won him recognition as one of the nation's outstanding historians.

Some other graduates achieved more local fame. Augustus Longstreet Hull, a grandson of the Reverend Hope "Broadaxe" Hull and a graduate of the class of 1866, served for years as secretary of the trustees and treasurer of the university. His *Annals of Athens, Georgia* and *A Historical Sketch of the University of Georgia* are still valuable source books. Thomas W. Reed (A.M. 1888, B.L. 1889) edited the *Athens Banner*. In 1909 he became treasurer of the university in the place of Hull, who had just died. In the 1920s the Reed family moved into Waddel Hall, and he continued his supervisory and advisory work until 1945. In the last five years of his life he wrote a detailed, informal history of the university that is available in the Special Collections section of the library in nineteen typewritten volumes.

Moses Gershon Michael, a Jewish youngster from Jefferson, graduated in 1878 at the age of fifteen. He and a brother founded Michael Brothers department store, one of the largest businesses in the Athens area. Michael contributed generously to the university over the years and served as the first president of the Athletic Board. In the 1940s his sons, who also attended the university, established in his memory the Michael awards for outstanding faculty research. Other Jewish students came to the university, mainly from Savannah, Atlanta, Augusta, and Athens; the university did not employ the kind of quota system used so relentlessly by many schools in the nation. The state of Georgia was certainly not free of anti-Semitism, but by the early twentieth century a few Jewish students graduated almost every year at the university.

The war with Spain in 1898 brought fame to a few alumni. Many university men volunteered to fight, donning the dark blue uniforms their fathers had fought against, but casualties were light in what Colonel Theodore Roosevelt (whose mother was a Georgian) called a "splendid little war." Two Georgia men became popular heroes. Albon Chase Hodgson entered the university in 1868 but soon transferred to the United States Naval Academy, where he graduated with first honors in 1877. A lieutenant commander when the war started, he was the navigator on the American flagship, the *Brooklyn*, when the Spanish fleet was smashed at Santiago, Cuba. Thomas M. Brumby entered the university in 1874 but, like Hodgson, soon transferred to Annapolis, graduating in 1879. He was with Admiral Dewey at Manila Bay and was credited by one reporter with suggesting the strategy that led to the dramatic American victory. More important, Lieutenant Brumby, the son of a Confederate officer, went ashore and planted the American flag over Manila. He reported proudly, "A United States regimental band . . . played the 'Star-Spangled Banner.' . . .You could hear the cheers from the ships as the Spanish flag came down and ours went up, and a salute from all our ships greeted the hoisting of Old Glory." Even though Hodgson and Brumby were graduates of Annapolis, they were hailed as true alumni of the university. The Civil War had ended at last; Old Glory was Georgia's flag again as the university moved into the twentieth century.

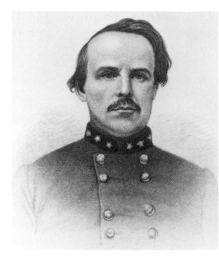

Left: Francis S. Bartow was first honor graduate of the university in 1835. He successfully practiced law in Savannah and was a leading secessionist at the convention that took Georgia out of the Union in January 1861. After brief service in the Confederate Congress, he took the first Georgia regiment to Virginia. At the First Battle of Manassas in June, Colonel Bartow led five regiments.

His troops were decimated, and Bartow himself fell at the very moment of victory. He was hailed as one of the Confederacy's first heroes, and Cass County (named for a Yankee politician) was renamed in his honor.

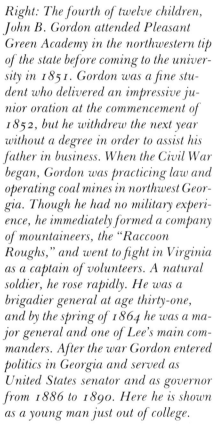

Right: The fourth of twelve children, John B. Gordon attended Pleasant Green Academy in the northwestern tip of the state before coming to the university in 1851. Gordon was a fine student who delivered an impressive junior oration at the commencement of 1852, but he withdrew the next year without a degree in order to assist his father in business. When the Civil War began, Gordon was practicing law and operating coal mines in northwest Georgia. Though he had no military experience, he immediately formed a company of mountaineers, the "Raccoon Roughs," and went to fight in Virginia as a captain of volunteers. A natural soldier, he rose rapidly. He was a brigadier general at age thirty-one, and by the spring of 1864 he was a major general and one of Lee's main commanders. After the war Gordon entered politics in Georgia and served as United States senator and as governor from 1886 to 1890. Here he is shown as a young man just out of college.

Left: Stephen Vincent Benet, the university's only Union soldier during the Civil War. In 1844, after prep school in Virginia, Benet entered the junior class at Georgia. Before graduating he transferred to West Point as Florida's first appointee, graduating in 1849. He remained in the regular army as an ordnance officer, and in 1874 he became chief of ordnance of the United States Army. He received an honorary M.A. from Georgia in 1855. On May 6, 1933, his grandson and namesake, a famous American poet, came to Athens on Alumni Day to present this painting by Henri Royer of Paris to the university. He read a long new poem honoring General Benet and "those men who, on each side, fought for the thing they loved and lived or died to prove its honor then." (Courtesy of the Georgia Museum of Art.)

Right: William G. Delony, class of 1846, became a lawyer, married, and settled down to bring up a family. When the Civil War began, he recruited a company of cavalrymen and rode off to fight in Virginia. Quickly he became an aggressive, instinctive warrior, a first-class officer. Brave to the point of recklessness, he fought in one skirmish and battle after another. In the fall of 1863 he was wounded and captured, and he died a few weeks later in a Union army hospital in Washington. Many years later a Union veteran who had befriended the colonel in the hospital wrote Delony's grown daughter: "Every one in the ward was very favorably impressed by his fine personal appearance and gentlemanly bearing. . . . Your father . . . said 'The doctors tell me that the chances are against me . . . and I have called you over to read to me from the Bible.' . . . I . . . had read (I think) about ten verses when he burst into tears and said 'Oh I could die in peace I could die in peace if I was only home with my wife and children: but it is so hard to die here far from home and among strangers." (Photograph from These Men She Gave, by John F. Stegeman.)

The first engineering class, 1868. As early as the 1830s there was talk of establishing a school of engineering at the university, but only a few isolated classes were taught before the Civil War. After the war a degree in "civil and mining engineering" was granted. Here Professor Leon Henri Charbonnier (with arms folded) poses with students: left to right, G. D. Harris, W. W. Kollock, J. J. Nevitt, P. H. Harris, A. J. Orr, and J. F. Kollock. Charbonnier arrived at the university as professor of mathematics and engineering in 1861 and remained until he retired in 1898. A graduate of the French military academy at St. Cyr, he was commander of the cadets corps as well.

Facing page, above: University High School, completed in 1862. As part of the reorganization of 1859, a "Collegiate Institute" was planned for freshmen and sophomores north of Athens away from the main campus. Because of strong opposition from underclassmen, the institute became a preparatory school for the university, called University High School. The high school stayed open throughout the war. Also called Rock College because it was made of crushed rock and concrete, it served as a school for Confederate veterans not prepared for regular college work, and later it was used as an experimental farm by the State College of Agriculture and the Mechanic Arts. In 1891, it became Gilmer Hall, a women's dormitory at the State Normal School, which grew steadily around it. In 1932 the university assumed control again, and the Normal School became the Coordinate Campus for freshman and sophomore women (who did not like the arrangement any more than the men had in 1859). Finally in 1954 the women went back to the main campus, and the United States Navy Supply Corps School took over the campus and demolished the building. This photograph, from Davis's Souvenir Album, was taken around 1875.

Facing page, below: Moore College was designed by Professor Leon Henri Charbonnier, built by M. B. McGinty, and named for Dr. Richard Moore, who led the Athens fund drive. In this photograph, taken soon after the completion of Moore College in 1874, the unique late French Renaissance building stands in the bare red clay with no more landscaping than the rest of the campus. It served as the home of the State College of Agriculture and the Mechanic Arts until early in the twentieth century. Other programs that have been housed in Moore College include physics, engineering, astronomy, and romance languages.

With so few extracurricular activities available on campus, some students organized small musical groups. This quartet posing in the 1880s at Clifton's studio includes, upper left, Charles H. Herty (Ph.B. 1886) and, lower left, Charles Morton Strahan, who received a degree in civil and mining engineering in 1883. After receiving his Ph.D. from Johns Hopkins, Herty taught chemistry at the University of Georgia from 1891 to 1902. He introduced football, basketball, and intercollegiate sports in general to the campus, and the athletic field behind New College was named for him. Herty's friend Strahan never left the campus. As soon as he graduated, he became a tutor in chemistry. In 1890 he succeeded David C. Barrow as head of the civil engineering department, a post he held for forty-three years. In 1934, when that department was moved to Georgia Tech, Strahan shifted to mathematics and taught on at Georgia until he retired in 1945. He taught at the university for sixty-two consecutive years, an unbreakable record. He further left his mark on the campus by designing structures like the Academic Building and Terrell Hall. (Courtesy of the Special Collections Department, Woodruff Library, Emory University.)

Facing page: The university's cadet corps stands in formation on the athletic field. The first photograph (courtesy of the Atlanta Historical Society), taken about 1890, shows New College, Old College, and at the far right the antebellum faculty house known as the Strahan House, which was torn down in the 1960s to make way for the expansion of the law school. The second photograph, taken about ten years later, shows, left to right, the Library Building, the Ivy Building, Demosthenian Hall, and the Chapel, which kept its cupola until 1913.

Telamon Cuyler Smith (1873–1951) attended the university only one year as a law student, but the photographs he took during the 1892–93 session furnish a valuable record of the school as it neared the end of its first century of operation. In 1905 he dropped his last name in favor of his mother's family name, Cuyler. Over the years he traveled all over the world, and he dabbled in journalism, music, art, sports, history, and even diplomacy. An old-fashioned southern gentleman and a talented dilettante, Cuyler never wavered in his support of the university. His historical and photographic collections remain in the Special Collections Division of the University of Georgia Libraries. This portrait was painted in 1905 by W. H. L. Cox and now hangs on the third floor of the law school.

Facing page, above: Georgia's first football team, 1892. Under the leadership of Charles H. Herty, class of 1886 and instructor in chemistry, this first team played only two games, beating Mercer and losing to Auburn. The captain of the team was Alfred O. Halsey (class of 1893, top left) who was honored at the halftime of the Tech-Georgia game in 1934. During the first Tech game, played early in 1893, George Shackleford (fourth from left on top row) engaged in an epic battle with the Tech star, Leonard Wood, a captain stationed at Fort McPherson. Tech overwhelmed Georgia 28–6.

Facing page, below: The first issue of the Pandora *in 1886 carried only three photographs: one page with head shots of the nine faculty, one page with head shots of the sixteen fraternity men who edited the* Pandora, *and one page of campus scenes with no caption or explanation. This photograph shows in the center Moore College, a new campus showpiece designed by Professor Leon Henri Charbonnier, built in*

1874 with twenty-five thousand dollars contributed by citizens of Athens, and named for Dr. Richard Moore, who led the fund drive. The upper left and lower right sections show equipment for the engineering and physics departments, which remained in Moore College until 1959. The upper right shows the inside of the library in the Library Building (now the side of the Academic Building nearest Broad Street), and the lower left shows the Chapel, which was frequently used to symbolize the university, with part of Demosthenian Hall by its side.

Telamon Cuyler Smith and a friend study after classes. This spartan class-room in the Ivy Building was typical of the no-frills University of Georgia.

The law school required its applicants to be eighteen (and, of course, male and white) but had no other entrance requirements. Operating out of two large rooms in the Ivy Building, it offered a one-year course of study and

had about forty students in residence. By 1898 it had taught 491 students. This photograph was taken by Tela-mon Cuyler.

*The library in 1893. The Library
Building was completed in 1862, but
the library itself was only one fifty-
by sixty-foot room on the second floor.
This photograph was taken by Telamon Cuyler in 1893, when the university had almost thirty thousand volumes and the entire second floor had
been converted to library use. Many of
the school's books were still kept in
departmental areas, so the library itself
was not overcrowded. The uncata-
logued volumes were shelved by subject
matter, and small signs at the top of
the stacks guided the reader to the
proper area.*

Students taking a break at a soda shop, 1893. Here, from left to right, are Samuel Rutherford (B.L. 1893), later a congressman: "Big" Smith, a football player; Thomas W. Hardwick (B.L. 1893), governor of Georgia from 1921 to 1923; William B. Armstrong, later a doctor in Atlanta; and Richard S. Hunter of West Virginia, who became the superintendent of a coal mine. Photograph by Telamon Cuyler.

In 1893 students were still required to attend a service in the Chapel every day, and the building had no difficulty accommodating a student body of about two hundred. Most of the numerous fistfights on campus erupted after chapel or literary-society meetings. Here students gather outside the Chapel, with many sporting traditional black derby hats. To the right is Demosthenian Hall. Photograph by Telamon Cuyler.

From the beginning of the university some students roomed in town rather than in the dormitories. This photograph taken in 1893 by Telamon Cuyler shows a student's room in a boardinghouse.

A marathon card game in 1893. On and off campus, students played cards frequently, and by the 1890s university officials tended to look the other way. Here in a dormitory five well-fortified students play poker on and on in an endurance contest. Photograph by Telamon Cuyler.

Above: In 1893 the Demosthenians and Phi Kappas cooperated to produce a campus newspaper, the Red and Black, *and the first board of editors posed proudly for a formal portrait. After a brief suppression, the Athletic Association took control in 1896. The paper continued its somewhat erratic course through the twentieth century. It became a completely independent newspaper in 1980 and moved off campus to offices in town. (Courtesy of Kenneth Kay.)*

Facing page, above: Field Day began after the Civil War as the only authorized university athletic event, and it was held every spring as a strictly local affair. Here on April 30, 1893, spectators arrive at the town's fairgrounds (roughly at the location of the university's modern track on the south campus). After the track and field events, wrestling, and the traditional chasing of the greased pig, participants joined spectators in a big picnic.

Facing page, below: The officers of the cadet corps stand in front of the Ivy Building with their flag leaning against the door. Third from the right on the front row is Charles M. Snelling, a graduate of the Virginia Military Institute who came to Georgia as a professor of mathematics and also relieved Professor Charbonnier as commandant of cadets. One of the Virginia-Maryland group that came to Georgia in the late nineteenth century, he worked his way up the administrative ladder to succeed David C. Barrow as chancellor in 1926. He became the first chancellor of the University System in 1932. Just to the left of Snelling is Harry Hodgson, who graduated in 1893, became a successful Athens businessman, and played a major role in university fund drives over the years.

*Above: Early in the 1890s the Thalian
Drama Club was organized, and soon
the Blackfriars followed. In this picture
taken about 1894 the Thalians pose before a performance; clearly the coming
of women students in 1918 would
make casting easier.*

*Facing page, below: The graduating
class of 1894 poses in front of the Cha-
pel. On the front row are faculty mem-
bers, from left to right, John P. Camp-
bell, B. F. Riley, Cyprian P. Willcox,
Chancellor William E. Boggs, Leon H.
Charbonnier, David C. Barrow,
Henry Clay White, and Charles H.
Herty. On the second row are five
junior faculty members, beginning
third from left, Oscar Sheffield, Wil-
liam D. Hooper, John Morris, Jesse
Coates, and Charles M. Strahan.
Missing are Willis H. Bocock, John H.
T. McPherson, and Charles M.
Snelling.*

Right: Organizations and clubs came and went rapidly at the university. The 1898 Pandora *gave full coverage to social groups like Yukpali, ETK Century Class Club, and Coxey's Army ("Away with prosperity and the inventor of labor. On to Watkinsville.") and to more serious organizations like the Mandolin and Banjo Club. But only a year later all four had vanished, as this cartoon demonstrates. The* Bumble Bee *was an underground student newspaper that periodically surfaced to attack some aspects of campus life only to be suppressed by the administration. As the large tombstone in the foreground indicates, it would return to the attack in the future. (Pen-and-ink drawing from the 1899* Pandora.)

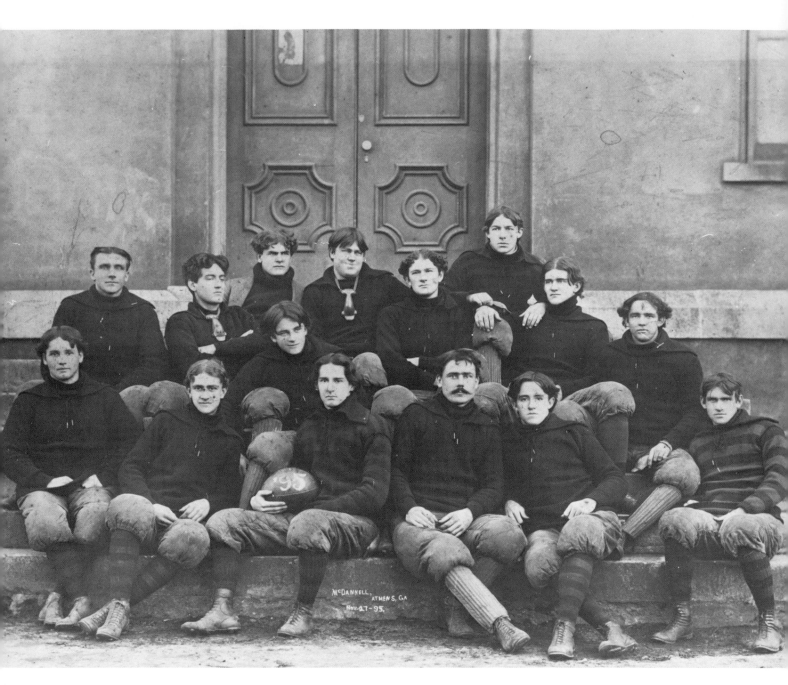

The 1895 football team, coached by Glenn S. "Pop" Warner of Cornell (third from left on top row), won only three of seven games, but the next year the Georgia team defeated Wofford, North Carolina, Sewanee, and Auburn, and lost none. Then Warner moved north to coach Jim Thorpe and the Carlisle Indians, Pittsburgh, and Sanford and win recognition as one of the game's greatest coaches. As the picture shows, protective padding is primitive, and the nose and mouth guards shown hanging around the necks of several players gave little protection against the kind of head injury that killed running back Von Gammon just two years later. (Courtesy of Butts-Mehre Heritage Hall.)

Left: Richard Vonalbade "Von" Gammon played fullback for a Georgia team that won its first two games over Clemson and Georgia Tech in 1897. The third game, against Virginia, was played in Atlanta on October 30. Early in the second half Gammon sustained a severe concussion in a pileup. He died at Grady Hospital a few hours later. The legislature quickly voted to abolish collegiate football, but Gammon's mother defended the game, "the most cherished object of his life," and the bill was not signed by Governor William Y. Atkinson, a Georgia graduate and a trustee.

Below: Dressed in a variety of uniforms, the substitutes for the 1898 football team line up in the T formation on the edge of Herty Field. Photograph by William Munroe White. (Courtesy of William E. White.)

Above: Baseball on Herty Field, circa 1899. William Munroe White took this photograph from a side window of Old College. To the right is New College and to the left Moore College, which was built in 1874. Herty Field was named for Professor Charles H. Herty, who brought intercollegiate athletics to the university in the early 1890s. The school had no other athletic field, and here football games were played until 1911. (Courtesy of William E. White.)

Facing page, below: A few outstanding juniors delivered brief speeches at every commencement, and selection for this was a significant achievement. Here the junior orators for 1899 pose in high spirits. The student who took the photograph, William Munroe White, is on the far right of the middle row. (Courtesy of William E. White.)

Left: The campus janitors pose on the steps of the Chapel in 1896. Not until the 1960s did blacks become part of the university's student body or faculty.

Above: Lucy Cobb students leave the Chapel, circa 1899. Lucy Cobb Institute was established in 1858. At first it was called Athens Female High School, but it was soon renamed in memory of Thomas R. R. Cobb's daughter, who had died of scarlet fever. Lucy Cobb educated the daughters of the well-to-do. Under Principal Mildred Rutherford the young women (sometimes called "goats" in honor of the school mascot) were carefully chaperoned, especially when they visited the university. Photograph by William Munroe White. (Courtesy of William E. White.)

Facing page, below: Posing near Old College with a visitor from Trinity College, members of the baseball team relax. Photograph by William Munroe White. (Courtesy of William E. White.)

Left: Joseph Lustrat, the third Frenchman to teach at the University of Georgia, was a professor of Romance languages from 1897 until his death in 1927. Here, around the turn of the century, Professor Lustrat poses with his wife, Marie, and their children (left to right) Marie, Renée, and Eleanor. Their house is now the office of the president of the university.

ENGINEERING AND DRAWING ROOM.

LAW CLASS ROOM.

UNIVERSITY MESS HALL.

CHEMISTRY LECTURE ROOM.

LIBRARY.

Above: Photographs from Hajo's
Athens, Ga. *show classrooms in*
1900. Clockwise from the upper left,
Moore College, the Ivy Building, the
Library, and Science Hall, and in the
center the dining room in Denmark
Hall.

Facing page, below: Largely funded by the New York philanthropist George I. Seney, the Seney-Stovall Chapel at Lucy Cobb Institute was dedicated in 1885. From 1931, when the bankrupt school was taken over by the university, until the completion of the Fine Arts Building in 1941, dramatic performances were presented there. Then the building languished for years. Its restoration was completed in 1997, crowning a monumental effort of more than a decade to save the entire Lucy Cobb complex, which then served as the home of the

Carl Vinson Institute of Government. This photograph shows the chapel set up for a musical concert at a time when Georgia men could attend only as visitors.

Above: Georgia and Georgia Tech trackmen pose for William Munroe White during a meet at Herty Field about 1899. In the background beyond the screen is the west side of Old College. (Courtesy of William E. White.)

Renaissance,
1899–1932

hancellor Boggs's resignation in 1899 marked the end of an era. Change was in the air as the Board of Trustees carefully considered whom to appoint as his successor. They chose Walter B. Hill, who combined the innovative flair of Josiah Meigs and the reforming zeal of Andrew A. Lipscomb. Hill began the transformation of a small liberal arts college educating a chosen few into a major state university committed to serving all the people of Georgia.

For the first time the University of Georgia was to be led by one of its own graduates (A.B. 1870, M.A. and LL.B. 1871), and for the first time since Josiah Meigs's presidency, it was not under the control of a clergyman. Hill was born in Talbotton, near Columbus, in 1851. After completing his education in Athens, he settled in Macon and practiced law with his classmate Nathaniel E. Harris, who later helped establish Georgia Tech and became governor in 1915. Hill became a very successful railroad lawyer, taught law at Mercer for several years, and campaigned vigorously against demon rum as a Methodist layman. He favored advanced education for women and sympathized with the concept of coeducation, which had already been implemented by many state universities. He also favored advanced education for blacks—but not with whites. Blacks had been subordinated in the South for a long time, and after the Supreme Court's *Plessy* v. *Ferguson* decision in 1896 the rest of the nation acquiesced. Even reformers and progressives like Hill had no interest in integration. White women soon began to attend the University of Georgia, but blacks would not enroll for more than half a century.

Hill was determined to shape a modern, progressive university in Athens. Somewhat reserved but relentlessly energetic, he was a talented executive with a first-rate mind honed by years of legal work. For the first time a leader of the university lobbied aggressively all over the state; indeed, Hill traveled throughout the nation championing education in general and the University of Georgia in particular. Understanding the importance of public relations, he gradually established ties with northern philanthropies while in Georgia he smoothly laid to rest the old antagonism between the university and church schools like Emory and Mercer.

Soon the legislature began to respond to Hill's determination and enthusiasm. With a population of over two million, the state could certainly afford more than its annual $8,000 contribution to the university, and Chancellor Hill's reminder that the Yankee government in Washington contributed far more than the state helped loosen the legislature's pursestrings. In 1900 the state increased its annual contribution to $22,500, the first real raise the university had received from the state since the Civil War but still not enough to finance all of Hill's optimistic plans.

Chancellor Hill also rallied the alumni. A weeklong centennial celebration in June 1901 attracted throngs of them. Hill invited Oscar S. Straus to deliver the main address. Straus, the son of a Jewish merchant, had been a boyhood friend of Hill's, but the family moved to New York City after the Civil War. Straus attended Columbia University, and then he and his two brothers built R. H. Macy into one of the nation's great department stores. Straus, delighted to visit his home state, brought along a friend, George Foster Peabody.

94

Walter B. Hill received his A.B. from the university in 1870 and an M.A. and a law degree in 1871. He practiced law with Nathaniel E. Harris, a fellow Chi Phi at the university and a future governor of the state. They became widely respected railroad lawyers, and Hill also won a reputation as a scholar of the law and a champion of judicial reform. An active Methodist layman, he was interested in prohibition, advanced education for women, and education for blacks. In July 1899 he became chancellor of the university; he was the first alumnus ever to hold that office and the first nonclergyman to lead the school in almost a century. At once he set about modernizing Georgia and making it into a real state university. Here he is shown soon after graduating from the university and as chancellor of the university with his dean, David C. Barrow.

The son of New Englanders, Peabody was born in Columbus only a year after Hill was born in nearby Talbotton. He went to school with Oscar Straus for a while, but he never met Hill. After the Civil War the Peabodys, like the Strauses, moved to New York, where George went to work at the age of fourteen. Peabody devoted his life to banking and became a Gilded Age millionaire. Like Andrew Carnegie, he spent his later years returning his riches to society. He gave much to black education and established the Warm Springs Foundation, which he recommended to his friend Franklin D. Roosevelt. He also became one of the University of Georgia's greatest benefactors.

Peabody and Hill met for the first time in 1901, and they quickly became fast friends. Peabody soon began to lavish money and attention on the university of his home state. Over the years he gave a quarter of a million dollars outright, plus all sorts of other unpublicized assistance. He occasionally meddled a little in routine operations, but nobody ever challenged his right to be the only out-of-state trustee, and nobody ever chided him for missing so many meetings. No alumnus could match the contributions of this New York financier who never even saw the campus until he was forty-eight years old.

The sudden influx of public and private funds made it possible for the university to construct several much-needed buildings. In 1900 the legislature appropriated forty-five thousand dollars for a new dormitory named in honor of Governor Allen D. Candler (a Mercer man) and a new dining hall named for Brantley A. Denmark (class of 1871), who had been a leader in alumni fund drives for years. In 1902 Peabody gave fifty thousand dollars for a new library building to replace the limited second-story area in the old building. Completed in 1905, the new library had room for sixty thousand volumes, though the university then owned only half that number. The legislature appropriated five thousand dollars for new furniture. The university hired its first professional librarian, Duncan Burnet, and Sarah Frierson remained as his assistant until 1910. Burnet frequently complained about "trifling loungers" in his domain, but he stayed on the job for over four decades, long enough to see the book col-

lection grow to more than two hundred thousand volumes and the building itself receive a thirty-five-thousand-dollar addition in 1937. In 1905 the old Library Building and the much-enlarged Ivy Building were joined by an elaborate central structure with a classical façade designed by Charles M. Strahan, class of 1883 and professor of civil engineering. The remodeled structure was named the Academic Building.

Even a sudden disaster could not stop construction. In November 1903 the six-year-old Science Building, between Phi Kappa and the new library, burned to the ground. The fire destroyed almost everything, including many records in Chancellor Hill's office on the first floor. The legislature voted to replace the underinsured structure, and in 1905, on the same foundation with the old cornerstone dated 1897, rose Terrell Hall, another Strahan creation. It housed the chemistry department for many years. The new pharmacy school operated in the basement for over thirty years, and the biology department moved to another new Strahan building, LeConte Hall, now called Meigs Hall.

This new construction filled in much of the old thirty-seven-acre campus, all that remained of John Milledge's original grant. Chancellor Hill directed the rapid expansion of the campus southward across a little creek called Tanyard Branch, which flowed southeastward from the old Botanical Garden through a little wooded valley that eventually became the site of Sanford Stadium. Peabody quietly purchased nearly four hundred acres worth twenty-two thousand dollars for a major expansion of the stunted A&M College, and increasingly active alumni contributed more land, much of it not connected to the old campus.

At the beginning of Hill's administration the university actually granted only a few degrees: the traditional A.B. and the one-year law degree were most popular, but some B.S. degrees were awarded as well as an occasional master's or bachelor of engineering. Hill immediately began to expand the curriculum. He appointed Sylvanus Morris the first dean of the law school, which added a second year of study. He established the School of Pharmacy in the basement of Terrell Hall. With the assistance of Peabody, who contributed the initial money for a

View of the campus, circa 1900. From left to right, Phi Kappa Hall (partly obscured by the town building that long housed Athens Refrigeration and Appliance Company); Science Hall, which burned to the ground in 1903 and was replaced by Terrell Hall in 1905; the west corner of Old College; New College; the Chapel, and in front of it the stump of the Toombs Oak; Demosthenian Hall with Moore College behind it; the Ivy Building; and the Library Building. In the foreground are four tennis courts.

forester, Hill established the Peabody School of Forestry.

He also started a summer school to improve the education of public school teachers. First funded in 1902 by Rockefeller money from the General Education Board, it was soon permanently supported by the legislature. Since many teachers were women, the campus finally received female students, but only with qualifications. The six-week summer session was not part of the regular university schedule, the women were not enrolled as regular students, and they had to room off campus—in town or over at the Normal School. Nevertheless, they did attend classes in university buildings and they did dine at Denmark Hall. Sixteen years later women enrolled as regular students at the university.

With the aid of Joseph S. Stewart, the new professor of secondary education, Hill prodded Georgia's growing high school system to offer more solid academic courses so that more students would be prepared to go on to college.

Gradually the better high schools adjusted their curricula so that their brighter graduates could enter the University of Georgia without taking the traditional entrance examination, and by 1906 enrollment at the university began to rise steadily, topping four hundred for the first time.

The faculty expanded steadily as well. For the first time a regular army officer directed the training of the cadet corps. Robert E. Park came from the University of Alabama in 1900; he headed the English department for forty years. Thomas Jackson Woofter, a Ph.D. from the University of Chicago, came in 1903 as professor of psychology and education and served for over thirty years. Steadman V. Sanford, a graduate of Mercer, arrived in 1903 as an assistant professor of English, but his main service over nearly forty years was as an administrator, in both the athletic and the academic side of university life. He eventually served as president of the university (1932–35) and as chancellor of the University System (1935–45).

Hill's most significant effort to expand operations and bring the university closer to the people came in the field of agricultural education. The growing federal funds that flowed to the university—always more than half of the annual operating budget—came only because of the existence of the A&M College on the Athens campus. Yet the university's agricultural operation was pitifully small—one professor and a few students shuttled around the campus and finally stuck back in Philosophical Hall, renamed Agricultural Hall. The traditional university soaked up the federal funds, allowing only a trickle to reach the impoverished agricultural operation. Chancellor Hill spun a fine legal argument to rationalize this longstanding ruse, but he also moved quickly to stop a growing movement to establish a new, separate A&M school like Clemson or Auburn. Working closely with James L. Conner and other legislators, he laid plans for a more independent and much more vigorous school of agriculture in Athens to serve the still predominantly agrarian state. In 1904, with funds provided by Peabody and a train furnished by Samuel Spenser, class of 1867 and president of the Southern Railroad, Hill took the trustees and some leading politicians up to the University of Wisconsin to see how a state university ran a first-rate agricultural operation.

Hill's health was not equal to the demands of his strenuous schedule. His friend Peabody realized that the chancellor's job was shortening his life and practically forced the Hill family to take a break and tour Europe, but it was too late. Soon after getting home, Hill contracted pneumonia and died in December 1905. His death left a void at the University of Georgia just as it was beginning to evolve from a college into a university.

The trustees quickly appointed Dean David C. Barrow acting chancellor. Six months later, at the commencement of 1906, they officially elected him chancellor, a position he retained for nineteen years. Like Hill a Methodist and an alumnus of the university, Barrow's roots went even deeper into the school's past. Three earlier generations of his family had served as trustees, and four of his brothers were alumni of the university. Barrow grew up in Athens in the

shadow of the university, just too young to join his older brothers in the Confederate army, and entered the freshman class in 1869. An intelligent and thorough but not brilliant student, he got into his share of trouble. A fight at a Demosthenian meeting ended badly when his opponent pulled a knife and cut him severely on the shoulder and cheek. Both combatants were expelled for a year, but they returned the following year and even became friends. Barrow graduated in 1874 with a bachelor of science degree and also a degree in civil and mining engineering.

He practiced law for a few years, and in partnership with an old friend in nearby Oglethorpe County he farmed for many years on the side. But soon he turned his attention back to the university in Athens. In 1879 he accepted a position as a beginning professor of mathematics. In 1883 he became a professor of engineering and in 1889 a professor of engineering and mathematics. In 1898 he was appointed dean of the liberal arts college, and he retained this key post throughout Hill's administration.

Students knew "Uncle Dave" Barrow as an administrator who really cared about them. They welcomed his appointment to the chancellorship with rallies and the firing of an old cadet cannon, and when George F. Peabody appeared, they pulled him and the new chancellor around town in a decorated carriage. Without faltering, Barrow continued Hill's crusade as the University of Georgia continued to grow at an accelerating rate.

Hill's plans to rejuvenate the A&M College materialized in the summer of 1906 as the legislature created the College of Agriculture with an appropriation of one hundred thousand dollars for buildings and equipment. One man was to be dean of the College of Agriculture and president of its parent, the A&M College (which consisted of the College of Agriculture and the College of Science and Engineering). A separate new board of trustees was to oversee the whole operation, but final control still rested with the chancellor and the trustees of the University of Georgia.

The A&M College remained a part of the University of Georgia—not one of the distant and practically independent branches like Geor-

gia Tech or North Georgia College—but never again would it be starved while federal land-grant funds were siphoned off by the traditional university. The restructured State College of Agriculture and the Mechanic Arts had a great deal of independence under the new arrangement, and it certainly found an independent-minded leader in its new dean and president, Andrew M. Soule.

A native of Canada, Soule graduated from the University of Toronto in 1893 with a bachelor of science in agriculture degree. He gained valuable experience as a professor and administrator at agricultural colleges in Texas, Tennessee, and Virginia, and he came to Georgia in

1907 after five years as dean of the College of Agriculture and director of the Experiment Station at the Virginia Polytechnic Institute. Soule took charge quickly, developing the new south campus, which lay just across Tanyard Branch from the old north campus. He was an able and aggressive administrator who fully exploited the increased federal funding available to agricultural colleges early in the twentieth century, and he also successfully sought more state funds—sometimes in competition with the parent university on the north campus.

He brought five key aides with him from VPI to coordinate his efforts, and by the time he re-

In 1908 Andrew M. Soule, president of the State College of Agriculture and the Mechanic Arts, chartered a special train to tour the state and demonstrate the modern agriculture then being taught in Athens. His "College on *Wheels" took its annual tour of the state several times before World War I, and several hundred thousand Georgians turned out at railroad sidings to see what was new at the university. Soule preached the gospel of scientific agriculture while his aides* *demonstrated its fruits on flatcars. Here Soule lectures a crowd of townsmen and "wool hat" farmers (facing page) while one of his aides discusses improved livestock breeding (above). (Courtesy of Mrs. R. M. Soule.)*

tired in 1932 he was directing a staff of 129 on campus and 220 county-extension and home-demonstration agents helping farmers and their families all over the state. Soule soon organized divisions of agricultural chemistry, agronomy, animal husbandry, extension, forestry, horticulture, poultry husbandry, and veterinary science. The Extension Service, established in 1914, drew reinforcement from the other departments as it spread its operation all over the state. In 1918 the Division of Home Economics emerged to accommodate women students, and Soule continued to add new programs as needs

and opportunities arose. In these early years most of his personnel had much more practical farm experience than scientific training, so he tirelessly stressed the importance of advanced academic credentials. A shrewd judge of talent, Soule hired some professors like Thomas H. McHatton (horticulture), Milton P. Jarnagin (animal husbandry), and Mary E. Creswell (home economics) who became leaders in their own right as the A&M College progressed.

Determined to reach and serve the ordinary people of the state as the university had never

done before, and hailing his operation as "the college with the state for its campus," Soule quickly set into motion a new program. In 1908 he chartered a special train to tour the state. Flatcars carried livestock, produce, and modern machinery, and Soule and his aides went along to spread the good word about scientific agriculture. The "College on Wheels" stopped at depots and sidings all over the state, and by 1917 several hundred thousand Georgians had turned out to see what was new and profitable in agriculture. In later years large trucks carried similar displays to the rural masses, who increasingly identified with the A&M school in Athens.

Soule led effectively for twenty-five years. Energetic, able, and dedicated, but not particularly tactful, he ran the A&M College as if it were a completely independent institution (which was largely correct). He left a trail of wounded feelings and bruised egos in his wake. Not even a salary reduction and a legislative investigation in the 1920s deterred him in what was, all in all,

a highly successful career in Athens. His free-wheeling style of management often brought him into conflict with the chancellor, yet he and Barrow met informally almost every Saturday afternoon and maintained a friendly personal relationship. Over the years they usually cooperated and always at least coexisted.

A similar relationship developed between the north- and south-campus faculties. The liberal arts faculty could not resist making occasional remarks about their colleagues in the "Cow College," and the agricultural faculty in turn sometimes hit back at the "old fogies" north of Tanyard Branch. These sentiments sometimes rose to the surface in faculty meetings. Yet these same people were also friends and neighbors in Athens, which early in the twentieth century had grown into a city of ten thousand with streetcars, paved streets, sidewalks and street lights, a striking new city hall (which is still in use), and a vigorous, segregated public school system.

On both sides of Tanyard Branch the professors had staked their futures on the greater

This unusual postcard view of the campus was taken around 1909. In the middle in the background stands Candler Hall, a dormitory completed in 1902. To the left is New College *and to the right the Chapel with its bell tower, which was removed in 1913. Between these two structures stand the bleachers at Herty Field,* *where football and baseball games were played until 1911. Back of the Chapel can be seen the crowded roof of Moore College, built in 1874. (Courtesy of Gary Doster.)*

University of Georgia. This fundamental unity was symbolized in 1914 by the marriage of Thomas H. McHatton, head of the Division of Horticulture, and Marie Lustrat, oldest daughter of the head of the Romance languages department. The bishop of Savannah conducted a proper Catholic ceremony in a new chapel that had just replaced the original makeshift one (T. R. R. Cobb's old law office, which had been the first home of the law school).

The north campus still absorbed considerable amounts of the increasing federal funds (which remained absolutely essential), but the south campus got a large share as well, plus considerable matching and supplementary state funds. The original state appropriation of one hundred thousand dollars led in 1909 to the completion of Agricultural Hall, copied from Townsend Hall at Ohio State University. In 1923 it was renamed James J. Conner Hall to honor the legislator who had led the drive for agricultural education. This modern, three-story structure—the first building on either campus with a central heating system—dominated the new south campus. An old two-story house called the Lumpkin House (originally the home of Wilson Lumpkin, the antebellum governor who removed the Cherokees from Georgia) stood awkwardly in front of the fine new building, but plans to tear it down were abandoned when someone noticed that the 1907 deed transferring the house and surrounding acres to the university specified that the land would revert to the heirs of the family if the house was ever removed. Thus the "Rock House" survived, serving over the years as a classroom, a dormitory, a library, home of the Institute of Ecology, and a computer center. Always too small for the growing university, it remains an antebellum redoubt resting in the shadow of a modern campus.

Conner Hall and its little satellite did not remain alone long on the original twenty-five-acre south campus. By 1928 the south campus had grown to two hundred acres and acquired many

In 1910 construction began on a building at first called Alumni Hall, and by 1912 it was being used as a one-story gymnasium with a swimming pool. Money became scarce and con- *struction was delayed, but after World War I a big fund drive began for a general activities building to be called Memorial Hall in honor of the forty-seven Georgia men who had died in the war. Construction resumed in 1921; this photograph was taken in* *late 1923. Completed in 1925, Memorial Hall became a center of campus life. It was enlarged by the navy during World War II and has served many functions over the years.*

new buildings. The university built the Farm Mechanics Building (1911) and the Agricultural Engineering Building (1916)—combined as Barrow Hall—and several veterinary medicine buildings, a greenhouse, and a few office buildings and smaller supplementary structures. A college farm (mainly for livestock) included a large barn and several sheds and cottages (all in the area of the modern Pharmacy Building). Professor McHatton, beginning the first landscaping program on either campus, introduced bermuda grass as an attractive alternative to the clay and weeds on north campus. Following a common practice of the times, he used twenty-five to fifty convict laborers, who were housed at a stockade nearby on the Oconee River. By 1920 a modern new dormitory with a gymnasium, swimming pool, and lecture rooms was ready for the new women students. Three years later it was named in honor of President Soule,

but around campus it was often referred to as the "coed barn." In 1928 it was supplemented by a large new women's physical education building. A building for animal husbandry (Hardman Hall) was completed in 1922. A large open-air amphitheater was constructed in 1922; it was filled in as part of the foundation of the Boyd Graduate Studies Building in 1967. And to accommodate summer camps for boys and girls in the booming 4-H movement a rambling wood-and-stucco barracks was erected in 1924 and soon named Camp Wilkins in honor of a local supporter. Nearby a creek was dammed to create Lake Kirota, named in honor of the Rotary and Kiwanis service clubs, which gave money for it. During the school year Camp Wilkins served as an inexpensive cooperative dormitory and dining hall for undergraduate men, and in the 1960s the psychology department used it as an isolation chamber for studies of the conduct of people in bomb shelters. It was leveled in 1966. In the late 1940s the pretty little lake and the campground with its winding trails and playing fields, which had become a campus retreat much like the antebellum botanical garden, vanished to make room for the College of Veterinary Medicine and the Agricultural Engineering Center.

Enrollment at the A&M College grew steadily. By the 1920s the college taught summer-school students (almost 2,000 a year) and special students who remained on campus only a few weeks before taking their new expertise back to grassroots Georgia, which was developing a more sophisticated, diversified agriculture. In 1927 the A&M College had over 330 fulltime students, most pursuing a four-year bachelor of science in agriculture degree. The college also offered (in order of popularity) bachelor of science degrees in home economics, in physical education, and in forestry; a doctorate in veterinary medicine; and a master of science degree in agriculture.

These A&M students also took courses in the traditional departments of the university, and they, like their administrators and professors, were also part of the larger, indivisible University of Georgia. Even their scientific specialties had roots running straight back into the antebellum curriculum. Indeed, Josiah Meigs, who first introduced an emphasis on science, would probably have heartily approved of what was emerging on the south campus. A new "city on a hill" was developing there, a complex of buildings and programs and dreams dedicated to the modern science and technology that would soon push Georgia and the South forward and project the American nation into a position of world leadership.

The north campus also grew under Chancellor Barrow's leadership. Not all of the federal A&M funds flowed to the south campus, and state funds increased rapidly over the earlier increases secured by Chancellor Hill. By the 1920s the total annual income of the university (north and south campuses) exceeded one million dollars. But the enrollment and responsibilities of the university increased correspondingly—from 383 students and 38 professors in 1906 to 1,664 students and 137 professors in 1925—and the school still operated very frugally. Like his predecessors, Chancellor Barrow

never addressed the whole legislature, but he did lobby key legislative committees to some effect.

Liberal in his commitment to continue Hill's reforms but rather conservative in fiscal matters, Barrow directed a steady expansion of the original campus. In 1908 the university established the School of Education, headed by Thomas J. Woofter, who also superintended the growing summer school for teachers. Howard W. Odum joined the three-man staff briefly and then moved on to the University of North Carolina to become a famous sociologist. Much later his son Eugene returned to the University of Georgia to establish a similar reputation in the new field of ecology. At first housed in New College—a catch-all building from the early days—the School of Education moved into George Peabody Hall in 1913. The forty thousand dollars for this new building came from the estate of a long-dead northern merchant who had prospered in England and whose 1869 will had provided that his fortune be distributed over time to a Southland devastated by the Civil War.

In 1912 the School of Commerce was established. It remained primarily a paper operation with new courses assigned to old faculty until 1919, when it moved into the law school's old quarters in the Academic Building (on the old Ivy Building side). In turn the growing law school moved across Broad Street to the rather large Athenaeum Building, which was purchased from the Elks for $15,500. That same year it added a third year to its required curriculum, and six years later it required two years of undergraduate work for admission. Like the whole university, the law school was trying to improve, and with 5 professors and 123 students by 1926, it was making progress.

In 1917 the Henry W. Grady School of Journalism emerged, with Steadman V. Sanford, professor of English, as its first head. In 1921 John E. Drewry arrived as an instructor, and before he retired as dean in 1969 he had developed a large, modern operation whose George Foster Peabody awards have become the Pulitzer prizes of radio and television.

The university also established the Graduate School to direct the slow growth of its graduate

Freshman agricultural students work at forges in a laboratory in the new Farm Mechanics Building (now part of Barrow Hall) around 1912. Vocational classes of this sort were still relatively new to the university.

programs. Willis H. Bocock, professor of Greek, became the first dean in 1910. Like many of the professors who had come late in the nineteenth century, Bocock found a home at Georgia and would teach there for fifty-six consecutive years, until a faculty retirement system was finally established in 1945. In 1904 friends in Virginia approached him about an administrative post at another school, but he declined, explaining candidly: "A fellow of my age [thirty-nine] must have measured himself, and must know his limitations. So far as I can see, if I can do any work decently, it is the work I have tried to fit myself for, these many years." Like their predecessors, Bocock and his colleagues on the north campus were primarily teachers, not researchers and publishers. They all carried a heavy load of classes, committee assignments, and other campus duties. The Graduate School, a locus for advanced scholarship, enrolled only around twenty-five fulltime students as late as 1925.

The traditional undergraduate program evolved a little more rapidly. Partially in response to rising enrollments at the less demanding A&M College, the north-campus faculty halved the Latin requirement to two years and made Greek an elective. Thus Bocock had more time for a deanship and later a course in international relations, and undergraduates enjoyed a more flexible curriculum. In-staters still paid no tuition, and others paid only one hundred dollars a year. Dormitories were five dollars a month for singles and four per student for doubles. Meals could be had at Denmark Hall for sixteen to eighteen dollars a month, and a few other annual fees were levied (athletic, eleven dollars; medical, five dollars; gymnasium, five dollars). Gradually the university was becoming more accessible to ordinary people (as long as they were male and white).

Additional new buildings on the north campus helped accommodate the growing student body, which had exceeded seven hundred before World War I. The Crawford W. Long Infirmary and the Octagon (a one-story frame building used mainly for summer-school classes) were rather modest structures, but Alumni Hall cost fifty-nine thousand dollars and contained a swimming pool and a gymnasium, even though only its ground floor was completed.

While new buildings were going up on the old campus, Old College, the original university building, barely escaped being torn down. By 1904 it had become uninhabitable, even for the hardiest students, but Chancellor Hill's plans for its removal were frustrated by nostalgic alumni and faculty. For a while Old College stood empty and neglected, but finally in 1908 Chancellor Barrow scraped up ten thousand dollars to restore it. The crumbling brick walls were stripped away and replaced with a new exterior as much like the original as possible. The old Franklin College building survived to serve again as a men's dormitory along with New College and Candler Hall. After World War I the citizens of Clarke County contributed the funds to construct Milledge Hall, the fourth men's dormitory on the north campus.

In 1925, Barrow's last year, Memorial Hall rose on the foundation of the unfinished Alumni Hall. This was the fruit of a massive alumni fund drive led by an Athens businessman, Harry Hodgson (class of 1893), a champion fundraiser. It netted over a million dollars, including one hundred thousand dollars of Rockefeller money from the General Education Board and sixty thousand from the university's old friend George Foster Peabody of New York City. This towering, light-colored brick building rested as close to south campus as Tanyard Branch allowed. It honored the forty-seven University of Georgia men who died in the First World War. In comparison with the Civil War, in which nearly a hundred Georgia men died when the school enrolled about the same number, the World War I dead totaled less than seven percent of the 1917 enrollment of 727. Yet the price of victory was still high, and the university remembered its fallen heroes.

Military training had been offered at the university since the 1870s, first under Professor Louis Henri Charbonnier, a graduate of the French military school of St. Cyr, and later under Professor Charles M. Snelling, a graduate of the Virginia Military Institute, but it had often been conducted rather casually. Early in the twentieth century the army detailed one of its own lieutenants to carry on the training. The students accepted the new leadership and new uniforms (khaki, a color that looked a lot like the old Confederate butternut), but military training remained somewhat relaxed in peacetime.

When the war started the Student Army Training Corps accelerated military training on campus. Many Georgia men hurried through school, received advanced officer's training at regular army camps, and then were quickly shipped overseas. More than a thousand university men served, many as infantry officers in the thick of the last great battles along the western front.

The war helped draw the north and south campuses together, and with the coming of peace a major change further blurred old distinctions. In September 1918 the university finally yielded to the prodding of organizations like the Colonial Dames and the Daughters of the American Revolution and admitted women as regular students. Even the relatively conservative universities in surrounding states had acted a generation earlier, but old Georgia insisted on moving slowly. Only the University of Virginia delayed longer.

Georgia women had begun to enter the university earlier. In 1903 women started attending the summer school for teachers, and in the following years outstanding female graduates from branch colleges at Dahlonega, Milledgeville, or across town at the State Normal School occasionally delivered a speech at the university's commencement. In 1914 Mary Lyndon received a master's degree in the regular session, and a few other women quickly followed in her footsteps.

By this time a few undergraduate women were being tutored by the university faculty while Chancellor Barrow looked the other way. Mary E. Creswell of Monroe graduated from the State Normal School in 1902 and stayed on to teach home economics and science. In 1910 and 1911 she quietly took additional science courses at the university. Then she became one of the first women in the United States Exten-

From *1911, when Herty Field back of New College was abandoned, until 1929, when Sanford Stadium hosted Yale in its inaugural game, Sanford Field served as Georgia's main intercollegiate and intramural playing* field. *It was named for Steadman V. Sanford, a professor of English who served as faculty chairman of athletics and in 1932 became president of the* university. *Designed primarily for baseball and football, its main stands followed the foul lines of the baseball diamond. In 1943 the navy constructed Stegeman Hall and its swimming pool on this site.*

During World War I the Students' Army Training Corps was organized on campuses all across the nation. Here *the Motor Transport Corps trains on south campus with some of the army's* *latest mechanized equipment. (Photograph from the Georgia State College of Agriculture Bulletin, 1919–20.)*

sion Service. In 1918 the A&M College made her head of the new Division of Home Economics, and the next year she received its first B.S.H.E. degree, thus becoming the first woman to receive an undergraduate degree from the university. In 1933 she became the first dean of the School of Home Economics. She served in that position until the end of World War II and taught on until 1949, when she finally retired.

The first Georgia women clustered deferentially in the home economics and education departments. For several years the *Pandora* presented graduating women only after all the male seniors had appeared alphabetically—in 1920 eighty-one men were followed by nine women with B.S.H.E. degrees. For many years, right up to the 1960s, women generally settled for the office of secretary, treasurer, or vice-president in campus organizations, leaving the top positions for men. This was partly because women usually made up only about a third of the student body, but even during the Second World War, when men were scarce on campus, women did not challenge the traditional dominance of men in campus affairs.

Even so, the coming of the women pro-

foundly changed the University of Georgia. Enrollment began to increase almost immediately; the student body numbered more than a thousand for the first time in 1919 and almost doubled during the 1920s. Mary Lyndon (M.A. 1914) served as the first dean of women, enforcing rules appropriate for southern ladies: no smoking in public, hats and gloves downtown, skirts and stockings on campus, bloomers for physical education, strict curfew regulations, no alcohol. And chapel was still required several times a week for all students. The university functioned as a parent away from home, and the women dutifully accepted this discipline. Of course, they bent the rules when they could as Georgia students always had, but open defiance meant that they could be (as old President Waddel would say) "sent away."

Soon women made their influence felt all over the campus. They enrolled in a wide variety of classes and started to major in a greater number of fields. In 1925 Gussie Brooks and Edith House graduated from the law school. The women students formed some new organizations of their own like the Pioneer Club,

At first most of the women at the university studied in the Division of Home Economics within the College of Agri- culture and the Mechanic Arts. Here home economics majors work in a hat- making class in 1919. (Photograph from Annual Report *of College of Agriculture, 1919–20.)*

Homecon, Chi Delta Phi (literary), the YWCA, the Student Government Association for Women, and Zodiac (sophomore scholars). Phi Mu and Chi Omega blazed the way for a host of sororities that bought houses along Milledge Avenue. The sororities greatly improved social life on the campus, and "Little Commencement," the formal spring dance, blossomed as the number of women increased. Women were welcome in many previously all-male clubs; the Thalian Dramatic Club's productions certainly benefited from women playing the female roles. The *Pandora*, the *Red and Black*, the *Agricultural Quarterly,* and the *Georgia Cracker* began to add women journalists to their staffs.

Yet women were not accepted everywhere. The two most prestigious campus clubs, Sphinx and Gridiron, held out stubbornly. The Reserve Officer Training Corps units of cavalry, artillery, and infantry were also off limits, but with the aid of the ROTC officers the women

did establish an active rifle team. They received standard army instruction and remained active over the years until regular ROTC programs finally admitted them. Women, excluded from regular varsity athletics, participated in intramural programs that included field hockey, basketball, baseball, swimming, track, horseback riding, riflery, archery, and Red Cross lifesaving tests. By 1928 this active program was centered in the new Women's Physical Education Building. Students who excelled received a monogram G, the equivalent of the men's varsity letter.

Men's athletics made much greater progress. By 1927 an extensive intramural program was supplemented with minor intercollegiate sports like golf, boxing, lacrosse, tennis, and riflery. The baseball team played a full outside schedule, as did the basketball squad. From 1924 to 1963 basketball games were played at Woodruff

A scatback slips through the line in a game at Sanford Field in the early 1920s. Long a powerhouse in the South, Georgia was beginning to attract national attention. By the end of the decade the university had a beautiful new stadium seating thirty-three thousand.

Hall, which was finally demolished in 1967 and replaced by the Psychology-Journalism Complex.

But football was king at the University of Georgia. Chancellor Barrow favored sports in general and football in particular. Since the death of Von Gammon in 1897, the game had calmed down considerably—rules were stricter and equipment more protective. Barrow felt that it was better to be "bruised up" on the gridiron than "burnt up" on the party circuit, and that football taught self-control and discipline and cut down on the number of fights on campus. Remembering his own campus fight, which had kept him out of school for a whole year, Barrow stressed this latter point. By the last years of his administration Georgia began to emerge as a football power. Great universities like Harvard and Yale and Chicago fielded potent teams, and Georgia began to compete in earnest.

After Charles H. Herty started football back of New College in 1892, a succession of new coaches slowly began to build a gridiron dynasty. Glenn S. "Pop" Warner came fresh from his playing days at Cornell to turn out a respectable team in 1895 and an undefeated one in 1896. Then he moved on to coach the Carlisle Indians (including Jim Thorpe), Pittsburgh, and Stan-

ford, and established himself as one of the all-time great coaches.

Georgia continued to make progress within the South, but national prominence would take a little longer. From 1910 to 1919 (with two years off for the war) Alex Cunningham, a Vanderbilt graduate, led the Bulldogs to a string of winning seasons and developed their first All-American, halfback Bob McWhorter. Then Herman J. Stegeman, a graduate of Chicago, coached an unbeaten team in 1920 and followed with two more winning seasons. George "Kid" Woodruff (a former Georgia scatback) took over in 1923. While continuing to operate a business in Columbus, Woodruff fashioned four winning seasons in five years as Georgia held her own with southern powers like Auburn, Alabama, and Clemson. Georgia Tech had already become the main rival, but this annual clash got completely out of hand and had to be discontinued from 1919 to 1925.

When Georgia finally tried to move onto the broader national scene, the team had to travel. Old, battered Herty Field had been abandoned in 1911 when Sanford Field was constructed on the site of modern Stegeman Hall. The new field was leveled and graded for baseball as well as football, and a covered grandstand seated thirty-five hundred spectators, but major northern teams still declined to make the long trip to

Well into the twentieth century the civil engineering majors continued to take field trips in the springtime to practice their new craft. Here a class gathers on a farm near Elberton in 1924. (Courtesy of Susan B. Tate.)

face an opponent with only a regional reputation. So the Bulldogs went by train to face powerhouses like Harvard and Dartmouth in 1921, Chicago in 1922, and Yale from 1923 to 1931, and 1933 and 1934.

Remembering the old connection, Yale always treated the visitors from the Deep South with courtesy and hospitality. Still, the young Georgians heading to Connecticut could not help but remember the past even after the Yale series ripened into an annual affair. Their train rolled north through a land still haunted by the past, and the names of old battlefields like Manassas, Fredericksburg, the Wilderness, Antietam, and Gettysburg stirred memories. The descendants of Johnny Rebs fought hard, but for six years they could not whip the Yankees from Connecticut. Finally in 1927 the Georgia Bulldogs defeated the Yale Bulldogs 14 to 10, and the tide turned.

By 1931 the Dogs from Dixie were clearly dominant. The *New York Sun* on Monday, October 12, 1931, described the weekend game before sixty-eight thousand fans in the Yale Bowl under a headline that proclaimed "Yale a Willing but Outclassed Outfit Against That Highly Polished Machine from Georgia":

"Joe-gah! Joe-gah! Joe-gah!" A small but vociferous group of Georgia partisans shouted themselves hoarse. . . . Georgia's case-hardened football veterans, their white cotton jerseys stippled with sweat and grass stains, trudged leisurely through the exit runway. . . . Beating Yale's green, inexperienced team was a mere formality as far as these rugged, polished veterans of three years' standing were concerned. . . . They didn't waste a glance at the score board legend: "Georgia 26; Yale 7." These figures didn't express their superiority. They knew they could have won by five touchdowns had their coach chosen to rub it in. . . . As the last Cracker warrior was swallowed up in the

111

"Uncle Dave" Barrow, chancellor from 1906 to 1925, continued Chancellor Hill's program to transform the school from a college into a true university, though he was often frustrated by financial restrictions. Much loved by the students, he became almost a tradition in his office in the Academic Building, as did his steadfast secretary, Sarah Cobb Baxter, a granddaughter of Howell Cobb. Though enrollment grew from under four hundred to over sixteen hundred during Barrow's administration, he and his secretary and a few other administrators handled all of the paperwork. (Courtesy of Susan B. Tate.)

dark portal, the blue-jerseyed Yale band came swinging across the cleat-torn field, its brasses blaring "Dixie!" It was a graceful tribute to the soft-tongued visitors from below the Mason-Dixon Line. A roar of pure joy greeted the stirring strains of that pulse-quickening battle march. . . . A rebel yell burst spontaneously from Southern throats. The echoes of that blood-chilling shriek still beat in the writer's eardrums as he pens this story. It's a sound you can't forget.

Georgia had already adopted "Glory to Old Georgia" as its fight song, even though it was one of the tunes Sherman's men had marched to as they swept through Georgia. Hugh Hodgson (class of 1915) had written the words and adapted them to a lively musical version of "The Battle Hymn of the Republic." It remains the university's main song, but for many years "Dixie" brought Georgia fans to their feet and unleashed their piercing rebel yells. The Bulldogs marched to both songs as they evolved from a strong regional team into a national power, capable of competing with the best collegiate football teams. The university became one of the nation's many football factories and began to attract many "subway alumni," fans who had never attended the school and in some cases had never even seen the campus. Many ordinary folks in Georgia began to show interest in the school that sent its Bulldogs out to do battle on the gridiron every fall, and Georgia increasingly became a university representing the whole state.

The graduation procession in 1926. With a total of 204 seniors (including 59 women) the graduation procession had begun to draw a large crowd to the amphitheater on south campus. The class of 1926 was described as the "largest class in the history of the University" in the Red and Black of June 5, 1926; enrollments continued to *climb steadily until the Second World War. (Photograph from the University of Georgia* Bulletin, 1926.)

The emergence of the football factory and the party school sometimes obscured academic and intellectual advancement. In 1909 the university's reputation was enhanced by President-elect William Howard Taft's visit—the first such occurrence since James Monroe passed through back in 1819—but Taft detoured over from Augusta mainly because as a Yale graduate he felt a responsibility to the school that for a century had boasted of its debt to his alma mater. In 1914 the university established the first chapter of Phi Beta Kappa in Georgia, and in 1923 Phi Kappa Phi, another honorary academic society, was brought to campus by President Soule. Town-gown organizations like L'Alliance Francaise (established by that good Frenchman, Professor Lustrat) began to spring up on the campus by the 1920s. The university also began to hold occasional conferences of scientists and scholars.

Nevertheless, the university remained a relatively isolated and obscure institution of higher learning. Like his predecessors, Chancellor Barrow stressed teaching, and the school's laboratories lacked the facilities for sophisticated experimentation. The library grew in the new building provided by George F. Peabody, who also periodically contributed books, as did Professor Ulrich B. Phillips. By 1915 over forty thousand volumes were properly shelved and cataloged under the Dewey decimal system. Even so, the library, like the science labs, lacked the resources to support most advanced scholarship. Many departments and the A&M College had separate caches of books, and only a very small amount of the annual budget went to the purchasing of new books. Professor E. Merton Coulter unearthed enough raw materials in southern history to begin to establish a national reputation as a publishing scholar, but most of his colleagues concentrated on teaching, the traditional mission of the University of Georgia.

Despite many problems, the university grew.

In 1925 the graduating class numbered 152 (24 percent women) plus another 27 in law (7 percent women) which was a larger total than the entire student body as late as 1891. The ranks of the alumni multiplied rapidly. Most remained in the Georgia middle class they came from. Successful people like governors and other politicians and wealthy businessmen who would have attracted attention in the early days usually got lost in the growing crowd, but Eugene Talmadge (LL.B. 1908) stood out. He carried a talent for speaking and organizing from school into politics and four times won the governorship. Gene Talmadge was the favorite of the white rural masses, and as long as the county-unit system gave disproportionate strength to that section of the electorate he was a power to reckon with.

A handful of other graduates also stood out. Harold Hirsch, the son of a German-Jewish immigrant, received his A.B. degree in 1901. From the day he set foot in Athens he fiercely supported his university, stepping willingly into every breach. Though not at all athletic, he filled in at center on a weak football team decimated by injuries. His only qualifications were size (160 pounds) and spirit (total), and Saturday after Saturday he took a whipping without wavering. After graduation he went on to Columbia University, where he received a law degree in 1904, and then he settled in Atlanta and prospered in law and business. He became general counsel and vice-president of Coca-Cola and served on the board of directors of Rich's and other big businesses. Over the years he gave more generously of his time and money to the university than anyone except George Foster Peabody. In 1912 Marion B. "Bubber" Folsom received an A.B. degree and then went on to Harvard, where in 1914 he received a master's degree in the new field of business administration. Later he became one of the chief executives at Eastman Kodak and then served as secretary of health, education, and welfare under President Eisenhower. In the early 1920s D. W. "Jimmie" Brooks received bachelor's and master's degrees in agriculture and the *Pandora*'s advice to "go into the teaching profession." Instead he became one of the nation's most prominent agricultural businessmen as president of Gold Kist Corporation and the

Cotton Producers' Association. Like Hirsch, he showered wealth and resources on his old school in Athens.

Robert Preston Brooks received his A.B. from the University of Georgia in 1904 and became its first Rhodes Scholar. After receiving his Ph.D. from Wisconsin in 1912 he returned to the university to teach history. In 1920 he became dean of the School of Commerce, holding this position for twenty-five years as the school grew into the College of Business Administration. After retirement he wrote *The University of Georgia Under Sixteen Administrations: 1785–1955*, which superseded Hull's and Reed's studies. In 1909 Young B. Smith received his B.S. and then went on to Columbia, where he got his law degree in 1912. After practicing law for a few years, he returned to teach law at Columbia. He eventually became the dean of the Columbia Law School. Francis G. Slack, who took only three years to earn his B.S. in 1918, received his Ph.D. in physics from Columbia in 1926. He became head of the physics department at Vanderbilt but returned to Columbia when the United States entered World War II. There he made a major contribution in the crash program to produce the first atomic bomb. A colleague in this crucial work was Eugene T. Booth, Jr., who received a B.S. (1932) and an M.S. (1934) from the University of Georgia and a Ph.D. (1937) from Oxford.

But the two most famous graduates of this era were both sons of alumni, and both came to the university a few years before World War I. Eugene Robert Black, Jr. (A.B. 1917) was a member of Chi Phi, Phi Kappa, and Gridiron, and won a Phi Beta Kappa key in his junior year when he was only seventeen years old. After brief military service he followed his father's footsteps into banking and rose rapidly, becoming a key executive in Chase National Bank of New York City. In 1947 he became associated with the World Bank, and by 1949 he was president of that bank, which was pouring billions of dollars into reconstructing and revitalizing the economies of the third-world nations. Only a few officials in Washington exercised more power and influence in the postwar era.

One of them was Richard Brevard Russell, Jr.

A fraternity party at the Delta Tau Delta house, 1920s. The fraternity oc- cupied the A. M. Scudder house, which was later demolished to make way for the main post office. (Courtesy of Susan B. Tate.)

(LL.B. 1918). As a student he was a member of SAE, Phi Kappa, and Gridiron. After briefly practicing law in his home town of Winder, he plunged into politics, and soon he was a power in the Georgia House of Representatives. In 1930 he was elected governor, the youngest in the nation and the youngest in Georgia's history. He reorganized the state government, including the system of higher education. In 1932 he was appointed to the United States Senate to fill an unexpired term. Reelected for six consecutive terms, he remained in the Senate until his death in 1971. By the end of World War II he had become one of the most powerful men in Washington, especially in the areas of agriculture and national security. Able and diligent, Russell might well have become president, but the postwar rise of the civil rights movement eliminated this southern conservative's chance

The Baum Festival in the late 1920s. With women matriculating in growing numbers and summer school develop- *ing rapidly as well, a number of summer pageants and ceremonies emerged. The new Memorial Hall provided a* *fine stage for such activities. These young women seem to be copying the old German Maibaum spring festival.*

for the Democratic nomination. Even his harshest liberal critics acknowledged his integrity and dedication, and bright, ambitious young senators (like the Kennedy brothers) always paid their respects to the reserved but courteous Georgian who had made himself a great American. Russell never forgot his old school and frequently returned for visits. After his death his extensive papers were entrusted to the university.

Another Georgia graduate achieved his own special distinction without leaving the campus. William Tate received an A.B. degree in 1924 and an M.A. in English in 1927. A member of Delta Tau Delta social fraternity, Gridiron, Sphinx, and Phi Beta Kappa, Bill Tate was also active in student government and was an outstanding distance runner. After a few years teaching at a prep school in Tennessee, he returned in 1936 as dean of freshmen and assistant professor of English. Over the years he be-

came a key administrator and something of an institution, much in the tradition of Augustus L. Hull and Thomas W. Reed. In 1946 he became dean of men, and for twenty-five years his tough but tenderhearted tutelage helped students learn to grow up. During the integration riot of 1961 and the peace demonstrations of 1970 his personal intervention played a major role in defusing explosive situations. By the time he retired in 1971 the university had become too large for the individual dean or professor to operate effectively, but Dean Tate still symbolized the university for thousands of alumni. In 1983, appropriately enough, the new student activities building was named in his honor.

While young Tate worked on his graduate degree, the university changed its leader for the twelfth time. After several previous efforts, the weary Chancellor Barrow, aged seventy-two, finally persuaded the Board of Trustees to accept his resignation in the summer of 1925. His

In 1927 most of the faculty and students of the law school, including a few women, posed on the front steps of the Athenaeum, their home from 1919 to 1932. Built in 1884 as a social club *on the north side of Broad Street on the present site of the parking lot of the C&S Bank Building (then the Holman Hotel), it was purchased by the university to house the law school, which had grown to about two hundred* *students plus three full-time and two part-time professors in 1927. Five years later the school moved back on campus into Harold Hirsch Hall, the nucleus of the present law-school complex.*

dean, Charles M. Snelling, was appointed acting chancellor in September, and the following summer the trustees made the appointment permanent. A native of Richmond, Virginia, Snelling graduated from the Virginia Military Institute in 1884 with "the degree," which did not exactly correspond to any traditional academic diploma but signified competence in mathematics and basic science. "Colonel Phil" came to the University of Georgia in 1886 to teach math and direct the cadet corps. Under Chancellor Barrow he rose to the deanship, just as Barrow had done under Chancellor Hill. Snelling was chancellor for only six years, but

his administration was crucial in the university's development.

A friendly, outgoing man with a large family, Snelling and his wife entertained frequently, but their delightful parties could not distract attention from hard times in the 1920s. Georgia's economy remained predominantly agricultural, and all over the nation farmers struggled to survive. The crash of 1929 plunged the entire nation into a deep depression. Georgia schools had been on a thin diet all along, but now budgets tightened even more. Young people who could not find jobs entered colleges in record numbers, so enrollment at the University of Georgia climbed steadily during the depression.

117

By the time Snelling resigned in 1932 enrollment had reached two thousand, out of a total state population of almost three million, including over a million blacks, who were still ineligible to attend. Faculty salaries, already low, were cut even further, and slashes in regular appropriations increased the general strain and left the campus looking even shabbier than usual. Occasionally the university had to borrow funds from private banks to continue operating.

Hard times had come, but some progress was made anyway. The active, growing Alumni Society began a drive to improve the law school, which had never gained much recognition beyond the state. With an inadequate library, an obsolete curriculum, and only one fulltime professor, it needed all the help it could get. The prominent Atlanta attorney Hughes Spalding (A.B., Georgetown, 1908; LL.B., University of Georgia, 1910) led the drive. In 1929 a new dean replaced the aging Sylvanus Morris, and two University of Georgia alumni with law degrees from Harvard became permanent faculty members. Four years later one of them, Harmon W. Caldwell (A.B. 1919), became dean of the law school, and two years later he stepped up to run the entire university. The other, J. Alton Hosch (A.B. 1924) took over as dean of the law school, serving until 1964.

A new building on the north campus across from Peabody Hall burnished the law school's reputation. On October 29, 1932, it was officially named for Harold Hirsch. In light of his past generosity, Hirsch was excluded from the fund drive that raised eighty thousand dollars, but, characteristically, he managed to donate many of its furnishings. Within the new structure the law library was greatly expanded and the curriculum modernized, and soon the law school received proper national accreditation for the first time.

Several other important buildings were added during this period. The Commerce-Journalism Building (which also housed Romance languages) was constructed with $215,000 remaining in the War Memorial Fund, and the Joseph E. Brown dormitory opened in 1932. But the most dramatic project required $300,000 to complete. Tanyard Branch, the little creek running through the valley separating the north

and south campuses, was diverted a little southward and sealed in a concrete tunnel, and over it gangs of convict laborers constructed a new football stadium seating thirty-three thousand people.

Sanford Stadium was dedicated on October 12, 1929, less than two weeks before the great Wall Street crash that ushered in the depression. Searching around for a prestigious opponent for the inaugural game, Georgia almost instinctively invited Yale. For the first time Yale agreed to play on Georgia's home field. A large crowd turned out to welcome them at the train station, matching the hospitality Yale had always offered visiting Georgia teams, but the warm reception the Yale men received in Athens turned uncomfortably hot in the new stadium as the southern Bulldogs trounced the northern Bulldogs 15–0, with All-American end Vernon "Catfish" Smith doing all the scoring.

This gridiron victory was soon overshadowed by the depression, but despite a deteriorating economy Chancellor Snelling made considerable progress beyond the new construction on campus. The Department of Fine Arts and Music was instituted in 1928 under the talented pianist Hugh Hodgson, who would serve as head for thirty-two years. The Bureau of Business Research emerged in 1929 but had to depend on outside funds from sympathetic businessmen. In 1927 the Institute of Public Affairs came to the university and for ten years brought in outside speakers, including some distinguished Europeans. A handful of students from nations like France, Germany, Italy, and China also began to appear on campus, often living cheaply in small rooms on the upper floor of Memorial Hall.

These young men from older, more formal cultures could only wonder at some of their American classmates' peculiar customs. Freshman men were hazed; they had to wear special caps, and before the football game with Tech they had to march through town in their underpants in the famous "shirttail parade." They could not walk under the Arch, and they faced kangaroo courts to answer for any transgressions. From seniors on down, students who lived in New College and Candler Hall waged pitched battles on old Herty Field. Parties,

Coach Harry Mehre's Georgia football team of 1931 compiled an 8–1 record, losing only to Tulane, before going by train to the Pacific coast to finish the season against powerful Southern California. The pregame hoopla included a team visit to Hollywood, where Georgia's quarterback and captain, Austin Downes (kicking), and All-American end, Vernon "Cat- fish" Smith, posed with Anita Page and Buster Keaton. The Hollywood treatment may have distracted the Bulldogs, who were defeated 60–0.

dances, and football games generated weekend madness. Campus elections pitted the well-organized fraternities and sororities against the Grand Old Party (no connection with the Republican Party) which was composed of other campus groups like Camp Wilkins and the dormitories. Only males ran for the prestigious offices. Most foreign students adjusted well to Georgia ways, and many, like Emilio Pucci, the Italian fashion designer, maintained ties with their old school long after they returned to their homelands.

An even larger group of outsiders came to the university for the first time from the North, especially New York and New Jersey, attracted by entrance requirements that rigidly barred only blacks and by low tuition and living expenses. World War II would bring many more Yankees to campus for military training, and from then on out-of-state students—nonsoutherners and non-Americans—became important elements at a state university that for over a century had remained isolated and provincial. Indeed, as Chancellor Snelling's administration drew to a close in 1932, the university and the state's whole system of higher education was modernizing.

Facing page, above: Gathering for the traditional class portrait on the steps of the Chapel, the class of 1900 numbers fewer than sixty. Photograph by William Munroe White. (Courtesy of William E. White.)

Facing page, below: This postcard, printed around 1900, shows two small cannons and one caisson in front of Agricultural Hall (originally Philosophical Hall). Peabody Hall was built to the right of Agricultural Hall in 1913. (Courtesy of Gary Doster.)

Left: The smallest and largest members of the 1903 football team, scatback Harry "Kid" Woodruff (120 pounds) and lineman G. A. "Baby" Moore (275 pounds). Harry's younger brother George (also nicknamed "Kid") played for the Bulldogs from 1910 to 1912 and then coached the team from 1923 through 1927. While driving up from Columbus to see his brother's team play early in the 1920s, Harry was killed in an automobile wreck. The Woodruff family contributed generously to a new gymnasium built in 1924 and named in his honor. (Courtesy of the Georgia Alumni Society.)

At the turn of the century the university was still a small school with fewer than three hundred students, and the population of Athens was little more than ten thousand. The intersection of Lumpkin and Broad (top photograph) was still peaceful, with the Chapel, the north end of Old College, and Moore College in the background.

Just north of the Arch is the intersection of College Avenue and Broad Street. The large building on the left in the photograph at bottom is the Commercial Hotel, remodeled in the 1920s. In the distance are the dome of the City Hall and the tower of the First Baptist Church, and far up College Avenue stands the Confederate monument, which was later moved to Broad Street.

This postcard photograph was taken soon after the Ivy Building and the Library Building were linked by a classical façade in 1905. In the distance stands the Arch, and beyond that can be seen the old hotel on the corner of Broad Street and College Avenue. (Courtesy of Gary Doster.)

Repairing Old College, circa 1909. By the time Walter B. Hill became chancellor in 1899, Old College (1806) was deteriorating, and he made plans to destroy the old building as part of his modernization program. An early effort at historic preservation held back the wreckers, but by 1908 Old College was vacant, no longer insurable. Then enough funds were collected to repair it, with the main effort directed at replacing the old bricks, which had crumbled badly. This photograph shows Old College laid bare and awaiting a new brick exterior. The repairs were soon completed, and Old College continued to house students until World War II, when it was extensively renovated to accommodate naval preflight trainees. After the war it became the main administration building for the university. (Courtesy of Susan B. Tate.)

By the early twentieth century fraternities were very strong on the campus. Their main activities included formal ceremonies like this Theta Nu Epsilon ritual in *1905* (below) and big weekends like the Kappa Alpha party at which the photograph at left was taken a few years later.

Facing page, above: Two Georgia cadets in summer dress uniform wait in front of their tent for inspection. Summer camp for cadets was held near Gainesville early in the twentieth century.

Facing page, below: The Georgia cadets march in a none-too-regular line on Herty Field in 1906. The building in the distance between New College and Old College is the new library, donated by George F. Peabody.

Above: Under President Andrew Soule the State College of Agriculture and the Mechanic Arts quickly began to reach beyond the campus to serve the people of Georgia. The horse-drawn milk wagon from the college soon became a familiar sight in Athens.

Below: Seen from downtown Athens about 1910, College Avenue and its streetcar line run right toward the north campus. To the right are the Commercial Hotel, the Academic Building, and the Chapel. In the background stands Old College, and on the left side of the campus are Phi Kappa Hall, Terrell Hall, and the library.

Facing page: In the first quarter of the twentieth century pushball became a popular intramural sport on many campuses. Two teams of about twenty men each tried to push the large inflated ball through the opponent's goal posts. Although pushball could be rough, the players wore only regular clothing. Here Chancellor Barrow, in the bowler hat, referees a game played around 1910; a few years later a battered contestant stands beside the ball after a game at Sanford Field.

Right: Henry Lee Jewett Williams was valedictorian of the class of 1907 and also captain of the cadet corps. Here he poses proudly in the army's new uniform of khaki, which replaced Confederate gray on the Georgia campus. He was also the university's second Rhodes Scholar; he studied theology for several years at Oxford and was ordained an Episcopal minister in 1911. Three years later he married Eleanor Priscilla Barrow, the daughter of the university's chancellor. When America entered World War I in 1917 he volteered for service. He was killed while serving as an infantry captain in France. Recently the elite 82d Airborne Division, the descendant of Captain Williams's old unit, honored him as the first man from the division to fall in World War I. (Courtesy of Susan B. Tate.)

Above: Standing near the Arch and looking up College Avenue, a Georgia student got a good look at downtown Athens around 1920. The city's first "skyscraper," the Southern Mutual Building, was constructed in 1908 and still stands, but the streetcar system and the drinking trough for horses have long since vanished.

Facing page, below: The first woman undergraduate with her diploma, 1919. Mary E. Creswell, a graduate of the State Normal School in Athens, took science courses at the University of Georgia and became one of the first women in the U.S. Extension Service. In 1918 she was made head of the new Division of Home Economics at the A&M College, and the following year she received her own division's first B.S. in home economics. Though Mary Lyndon had received an M.A. in 1914, Mary Creswell ended the exclusion of women from the university's main undergraduate programs. From 1933 to 1945 she was dean of the School of Home Economics, and she continued to teach until her retirement in 1949. She died in 1960. (Courtesy of the College of Home Economics.)

Above: Groundbreaking for Soule Hall, 1918. President Andrew M. Soule of the State College of Agriculture and the Mechanic Arts turns the first shovelful of earth for the construction of the first women's dormitory, which was named for him in 1920. Behind him to the right is Chancellor David C. Barrow (with the white beard and derby hat), and a little farther to the right with arms folded is Dean Willis H. Bocock, head

of the small graduate program. The woman in the center in a dark dress is Mrs. Soule, and next to her in white is Mary E. Creswell, who had just established the Division of Home Economics. The uniformed men on the right are "Rehabs," disabled veterans of the Great War receiving training of any sort, mainly at the A&M College. The white cottage would house ten senior women, and the other cottage would serve as a nursery school. The distant building in the left background is Jeruel Academy, a black school beyond the campus. (Courtesy of the College of Home Economics.)

The senior parade. Every spring before the "Little Commencement" dance
and the home baseball game with
Georgia Tech, the male seniors paraded at Sanford Field in all sorts of
wild, irreverent costumes. The sign
worn by the student in the photograph
at bottom on facing page refers to Sylvanus Morris, dean of the law school
from 1900 to 1929. In 1918 some of
the displays more than hinted that
Tech men stayed at home playing football while Georgia sent its men to fight
in France. The Tech series did not resume until 1925, when tempers had
cooled. Most fans enjoyed the digs at
Tech, but during the 1920s many objected to the increasingly outrageous
costumes and behavior. By the 1930s
the seniors, formally dressed with the
men sporting canes and derbys, simply
strolled around the field at Sanford
Stadium at the half of the homecoming
football game. (Photograph at top on
facing page courtesy of Anne and
Branch Howe.)

Facing page, above: ROTC review, 1922. Candler Hall, a men's dormitory, is in the background; in the forefront two officers watch the troops pass in review on Herty Field. (Courtesy of Susan B. Tate.)

Facing page, below: Almost as soon as women arrived at the University of Georgia as regular students in 1918 they organized a women's rifle team with the assistance of regular army officers on campus to train the men. The 1923 team poses in front of the Octagon, a wooden structure built about 1915 on the site of the Main Library parking lot. Used mainly as a small auditorium during summer school, the Octagon was torn down in the 1930s. (Photograph from the 1923 Pandora.)

Above: Three students study in a spartan room in one of the school dormitories in the 1920s. (Courtesy of Susan B. Tate.)

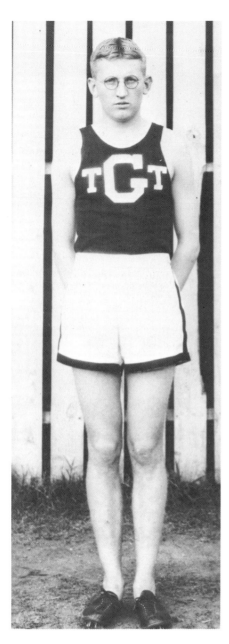

Facing page, above: The first women students at the university majored in home economics. Here in 1921 a home ec class judges poultry. (Photograph from the "Report of the President of the State College of Agriculture and the Mechanic Arts, 1921–1922.")

Facing page, below: Only six years after the first woman received an undergraduate degree, Georgia's women students pose on the steps of Terrell Hall. Their numbers increased steadily until today they outnumber the undergraduate men.

Left and below: A native of north Georgia, William Tate excelled in academics, politics, and athletics while a student at Georgia. He was an outstanding distance runner, setting records in the one- and two-mile runs and winning the state AAU cross-country championship in 1926. He received his B.A. in 1924 (Phi Beta Kappa) and an M.A. in English in 1927. After a few years teaching at McCallie School in Chattanooga, he returned to the campus as dean of freshmen and assistant professor of English. After World War II he became dean of men, a post he held until his retirement in 1971. For a generation he helped shepherd students through the university, and gradually he came to be a living symbol of the school. (Courtesy of Susan B. Tate.)

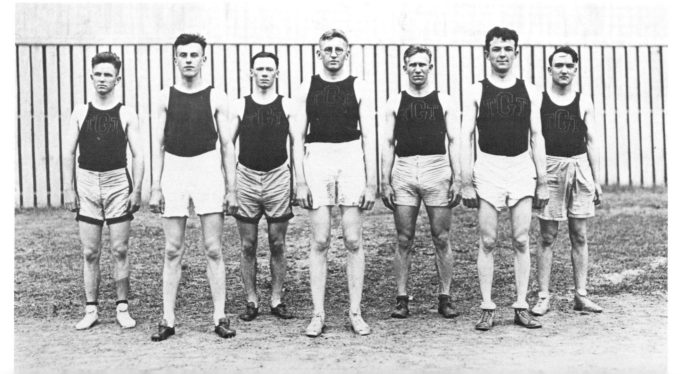

138

Facing page, above: Finally completed in 1925, Memorial Hall was dedicated to the forty-seven University of Georgia men who died in World War I. Sanford Field barely shows in the distance to the left of the new building.

Facing page, below: The dedication of Memorial Hall, Parents' Day 1925. Gathered on the front steps are, left to right, Andrew M. Soule, president of the College of Agriculture and the Mechanic Arts; C. H. Brent, a local minister; Chancellor David C. Barrow, who would retire before the year ended; the New York banker George Foster Peabody, the most generous benefactor in the university's history; Newton D. Baker, secretary of war under President Woodrow Wilson; and Dean Charles M. Snelling, Barrow's successor as chancellor. (Courtesy of Susan B. Tate.)

Above: Built in 1849 as the home of the president, this brick house lasted for a century. "Uncle Dave" Barrow was the last chancellor to live in it, and after he retired in 1926 it served the art and music departments and the University Press, and for a while it housed sophomore women. In 1950 it was torn down to make way for the new Main Library. This photograph was taken in the 1920s.

Built in 1924 by the students, this cabin was the headquarters of the Forestry Club, and it also served as an inexpensive dormitory without electricity for some of them. On Saturday nights it functioned as an informal dance hall. Here some students and a few faculty gather around the large fireplace in 1927. The cabin was demolished in 1956, and today only the massive fireplace remains on a wooded hill overlooking Lake Herrick near the intramural fields. (Courtesy of the School of Forest Resources.)

In the mid-1920s Conner Hall dominated the new south campus beyond Tanyard Branch. Just in front of it stands the Lumpkin House (or the Rock House), the oldest building in the area, and just behind it stands the first wing of the Farm Mechanics Building (1911). A little farther south along the road running toward the horizon is Hardman Hall (1922) for animal husbandry. Beyond that are a few barns, and the long, low, white structure to the left as the road fades away is the recently completed Camp Wilkins. On the far right next to the amphitheater is Soule Hall (1920), the women's dormitory, and to the far left are the three small structures that belonged to the struggling veterinary-medicine school.

Above: Harry Hodgson (class of 1893), a prominent Athens businessman, had been a leader in alumni fund drives for years when he received this loving cup in the mid-1920s in recognition of his efforts. To his left stands George Foster Peabody, a native of Georgia who made millions as a New York banker and then, like Andrew Carnegie, spent much of his later life giving it back to society. Though he had never attended the University of Georgia or even visited it until the centennial celebration of 1901, he poured money and other gifts into the school at a crucial time in its development. To the right of Hodgson is Chancellor David C. Barrow, who led the university from 1906 to 1925.

Facing page: Faculty picnic, 1920s. Standing at the left of the photograph at bottom are Joseph S. Stewart and his wife. Stewart, professor of secondary education at the university from 1905 until his death in 1934, was instrumental in improving high schools throughout Georgia and the South. He was also active in bringing professional opera singers to campus during the summer. It is possible that this picnic was in honor of one of the singers, perhaps the woman seated at the center.

Facing page: Construction of Sanford Stadium began in 1928 in the natural wooded valley between the north and south campuses. Machinery and equipment were still rather simple in the 1920s, and, as was customary then, convict laborers furnished much of the manpower. The bottom photograph shows prisoners in striped clothing loading mule-drawn wagons while Dean Sanford and others stand before the wagon on the right. Memorial Hall is in the background. The main engineering feat was to divert Tanyard Branch a little southward and seal it in a tunnel which would run under the playing field. In the photograph at top workers complete the concrete culvert while far in the distance stand the bleachers at Sanford Field.

Above: Soon after its completion in 1929, Sanford Stadium stands empty and peaceful in the little valley between the north and south campuses of the university. Already the playing field rests "between the hedges," which soon grew much larger. The stands also grew steadily, from an original seating capacity of 33,000 to over 86,000 by the late 1990s, and the graceful little fieldhouse in the background expanded as well. The railroad embankment in the far background served as free seating for some of the Bulldogs' most partisan fans until that end of the field was enclosed with additional stands in 1981.

ATLANTA GEORGIAN

Vol. XXVIII, No. 147 — Copyright, 1929, by The Georgian Company. Reg. U. S. Patent Office — SATURDAY, OCTOBER 12, 1929 — TWO CENTS Atlanta and Suburban Three Cents Elsewhere

GEORGIA, YALE READY FOR CLASH

40,000 Swarm Athens for Southern Grid Classic

U. S. INDICTS MANLEY'S DOCTOR

Charging he used perjury in conspiring to prevent trial of W. D. Manley, former Atlanta banker, on a charge of using the mails to defraud, Dr. H. Dawson Allen, of Milledgeville, was indicted on three counts by the Federal Grand Jury late yesterday.

With his physician disposed of by the federal indictment, officials to-day said Manley, the crash of whose 59 banks in Georgia and Florida was a sensation three years ago, probably will be brought to trial Monday.

The indictment of Dr. Allen yesterday climaxed three years of attempts on the part of the government to bring the defaulting banker to trial. Manley, backed by the doctor, steadfastly has refused to appear at a trial, saying he was not physically able.

REFUSED TO TESTIFY.

Last week, Dr. Allen was ordered before the federal grand jury to tell Manley's true condition. He refused to testify and was cited for contempt of court, at which time he gave facts on which the government's perjury indictment was based.

CITY GREETS ELI TEAM WARMLY

By TARLETON COLLIER,
Staff Correspondent of The Georgian.

ATHENS, Ga., Oct. 12.—Up here in Athens, the welkin is set in its ways. Almost any syllable you may utter, whether it be in sophomore math, where the aspiring devotees of Algebra undertake to apply the binomial theorem, or whether at the corner of College and Clayton the rowdy visitor seeks the purchase of a very thin pint, is apt to whisper back something approximating "wreck Tech," or a least "T.H.W.T."

Put today an unaccustomed breath is in the lambent autumn air. The burden of it is "Bet-cha-we-can't."

Yale's, the least traveled of major football squads, is here. Allen cleats are penetrating the bermuda carpet of Sanford Stadium for the first time. The Big Blue has come South, and Athens is in a frenzy of ostentatious hospitality.

TOWN ON ITS EAR.

The town, in words short and simple, is on its ear. Yale, headed by President Angell, and all its other dignitaries, arrived in Athens to the

GREAT CROWD ON HAND TO GIVE VISITORS GREETING.

One of the biggest and most enthusiastic crowds Athens ... picture shows the throng eager to welcome the visitors for ...

RED AND BLACK HOPES RISE AS EASTERN MEN ARRIVE AND PRACTICE

By JIMMY BURNS.

ATHENS, Ga., Oct. 12.—Ambitious to blaze their name across the national gridiron horizon, Georgia's Bulldogs this afternoon will spend all their physical stamina and exhaust all of their football cunning in the laudable endeavor to repel Yale's first invasion of the Sunny South.

Success in that endeavor would add the halo of victory to other features attendant on the dedication of Georgia's brand-new and handsome Sanford Stadium.

Georgia has only a slim chance of winning, yet the underdog has a habit of biting the hand that would conquer. That, coupled with the sheer brilliance of this city's greatest sport spectacle, has attracted a capacity crowd. When the two teams square off for the kick-off at 2 o'clock this afternoon every available spot in the stadium will be occupied.

Conservative estimates since the crowd at 42,900. There are seats for that many and, by use of standing room and aisle seats, the number will be materially increased. At any rate it is safe to predict that the largest crowd ever to witness a game in the South, outside of Atlanta, will roar a welcome to the kick-off.

An undercurrent of optimism was noted here yesterday afternoon after Yale had clicked through its workout on Sanford Field. There was nothing superhuman in the ...

Probable Lineup

YALE.		GEORGIA.
Hickoff	L. E.	Smith
Marting	L. T.	Rose
Greene (c)	L. G.	Maddox
Palmer	C.	Boland (c)
Lassoe	R. G.	Steffins

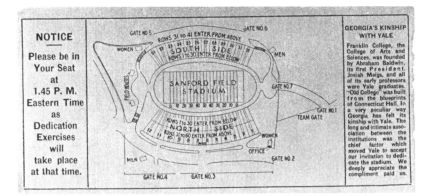

Above: In 1929 all Georgia waited expectantly for the Yale football team to make its first visit to the South and inaugurate Sanford Stadium. The newspapers covered the arrival on the front page, and the whole state rejoiced when Georgia won.

146

Facing page, below: The front and back of a ticket to the first game played in Sanford Stadium, October 12, 1929. Georgia had always gone north to play Yale, but this time Yale, still very conscious of its role in the establishment of the University of Georgia, agreed to come south for the first time. The tickets printed in Athens proudly acknowledged Georgia's debt to Yale and included a diagram of the beautiful stadium. The Georgia Bulldogs, led by All-American end Vernon "Catfish" Smith, defeated the Yale Bulldogs 15–0 to inaugurate the new stadium properly. (Courtesy of W. Frank Brookins.)

Above: In 1930 and again in 1931 the Bulldogs ventured north to defeat New York University, both times by the narrow margin of 7 to 6. Here Spurgeon Chandler gets loose for a short gain. Chandler, an all-round athlete who excelled as a pitcher in baseball, later became known as "Spud" Chandler, one of the stars of the powerful New York Yankees.

147

The third week of June was Women's Week at the University of Georgia. From all over the state women came to attend lectures and demonstrations by state extension specialists in nutrition, food preservation, clothing, arts and crafts, and other skills useful at home. Sponsored by the College of Agriculture, the camp was timed to coincide with graduation so that many of the women could watch their children receive diplomas. The women, photographed here in 1929, were housed at Camp Wilkins, a large barrackslike building of wood and stucco built in 1924 on south campus and named for a local supporter. During the rest of the summer it housed other special students and 4-H Club members. During regular sessions of the university it served as an inexpensive dormitory, mostly for agricultural engineering majors. It had kitchen and dining facilities along with its spartan living quarters, and it charged very low fees and accepted almost anything for payment. Camp Wilkins students developed a strong esprit de corps much like a fraternity, and their bloc vote could swing campus elections. In 1963 the camp served as a simulated fallout shelter for psychological testing, and then it was torn down to make way for the new Agricultural Engineering Building. (Courtesy of the College of Home Economics.)

The new Library Building, the gift of George F. Peabody, cost fifty thousand dollars. Five thousand dollars from the legislature provided for furnishings. Inevitably there arose some complaints about "trifling loungers" in the reading rooms and later, after women arrived, about "would be lovers" who came to the library not to study but to "jelly." This facility served the school from 1905 until 1953, when once again the library moved to larger quarters. The building then became the Georgia Museum of Art, and later it was used as one of the main administrative buildings.

Left: Hirsch Hall was completed in 1932 as part of a general improvement of the law school. Seen from the top of the new building's spiral staircase, law students gather in the main hall. The new facilities in this building soon led to the first proper national accreditation of the law school. (Courtesy of Kenneth Kay.)

Below: Campus beauties of the 1930s take part in halftime ceremonies at Sanford Stadium. (Photograph from the 1931 Pandora.)

Facing page, below: A group of law students and members of the Phi Delta Phi legal fraternity cavort on College Avenue in the 1930s. (Photograph from the 1931 Pandora.)

An outstanding student and athlete in the class of 1903, Sandy Beaver remained a loyal alumnus of the University of Georgia all his life. He served as a regent for almost twenty years. Though a longtime supporter of Governor Eugene Talmadge (class of 1908), he opposed the governor's purge of several faculty members, which led to a brief loss of accreditation by all the white schools in the University System of Georgia in 1941. A decade after Beaver's death in 1969, the trustees of his Riverside Military Academy granted the university two million dollars to be used to reward good teaching. Here in the 1930s Beaver, a striking, forceful man with Indian ancestry, chats with Grace McClatchey Sanford, wife of the president of the university.

The Modern Era,
1933–1984

Chancellor Snelling guided the growing university for only six years, but his administration ended with one of the most decisive developments in the school's history. In 1931 Governor Richard B. Russell, Jr. (LL.B. 1918) pushed through a reorganization of state government that was directed toward greater efficiency and economy. Included in this vast overhaul was the antiquated system of colleges, most technically branches of the University of Georgia but in reality independent competitors, each going after all it could get from the legislature.

Fortunately for the university, this aspect of Governor Russell's reforms was dominated by two Georgia alumni. Philip Weltner (A.B. 1907) chaired an Alumni Society reform study in 1929, drafted the final legislation in 1931, and then served on the newly created Board of Regents; Hughes Spalding (LL.B. 1910) presided over the reforms in the first two crucial years as chairman of the Board of Regents. Spalding remained one of the University of Georgia's main supporters, returning to the Board of Regents in later years.

The Board of Regents of the University System of Georgia was created to consolidate higher education in the state. Appointed by the governor, it replaced all of the old independent boards of trustees, including the university's, which had been in existence for more than a century. The Board of Regents had sweeping powers over the new, streamlined system of fifteen schools. The senior colleges were the University of Georgia, Georgia Tech, a college for blacks in Savannah, and Georgia State College for Women in Milledgeville. It also controlled the Medical College of Georgia; junior colleges at Dahlonega, Carrollton, Americus, Cochran, and Douglas; black institutions at Albany and Forsyth; and a two-year agricultural school at Tifton. By 1933 the regents received all legislative appropriations in a lump sum with no strings attached and then doled them out to the schools in the new system. The regents could abolish, create, or consolidate schools, and they could generally run things as they saw fit.

Spalding, Weltner, and five other University of Georgia alumni dominated the original ten-man and one-woman Board of Regents, and their chief executive officer, the chancellor of the whole system, was Charles Snelling, who resigned as the chancellor of the University of Georgia in 1932. The regents followed custom and replaced him with his dean, Steadman V. Sanford, who became the first official to bear the title president of the University of Georgia since 1860. The elderly Snelling was soon replaced as chancellor by Weltner, who in turn was replaced by Sanford in 1935. Sanford's replacement in Athens was the dean of the law school, Harmon W. Caldwell.

University of Georgia graduates continued to dominate the powerful Board of Regents and the less powerful chancellorship. President Sanford led the university for three crucial years, 1932–35, as the new regents directed sweeping changes. The A&M College was completely merged with the university, losing its last vestiges of independence. The Georgia State College of Agriculture and the Mechanic Arts became the College of Agriculture of the University of Georgia, and the proud, energetic Andrew M. Soule, now only a dean and no longer a president, retired after twenty-six

During his first administration, in the mid-1930s, Governor Eugene Talmadge (LL.B. 1908) visited the campus, where his son Herman received his LL.B. in 1936. Standing on the Chapel steps are, left to right, Robert Preston Brooks, dean of the School of Commerce; Governor Talmadge; Herman Talmadge; Steadman V. Sanford, president of the university from 1932 to 1935; and William Oscar Payne, professor of history and faculty chairman of athletics. During his first administration Talmadge opposed President Roosevelt's New Deal so bitterly that the university had difficulty getting federal building funds, and during his second administration, 1941–43, Talmadge intervened directly in academic affairs and caused the uni-*versity to lose its accreditation briefly. Herman, who was governor from 1948 to 1955, funneled vast amounts of money to his alma mater and played a major role in the postwar growth of the university.*

years of service. Across town on Prince Avenue the State Normal School became the Coordinate College for Freshman and Sophomore Women. Some young women had taken two years of college work at Lucy Cobb Institute on Milledge Avenue until that private school fell victim to the depression in 1931, but most Georgia women preferred life on the main campus of the university. Nevertheless, as freshmen and sophomores they had to live and take most classes across town from 1933 until 1954, when the United States Navy purchased the campus of the Coordinate College and established the

Supply Corps School there. The navy kept and renovated most of the old buildings but demolished the dormitory Gilmer Hall, which had been University High School (or Rock College) during Reconstruction.

The university's archrival, Georgia Tech, gained all of the engineering specialties outside of agriculture but in return yielded its commerce program to the university. The university's expensive veterinary-medicine division was abolished for "lack of interest," and its three small buildings were taken over by the

College of Agriculture. In 1946 the veterinary school came to life again in Hardman Hall and rapidly developed into one of the university's more prestigious colleges. The struggling medical school at Augusta remained affiliated with the university until 1949, when it became the independent Medical College for Georgia.

Internally the university changed a great deal. The quarter system was adopted, and freshmen and sophomores took required general courses (four in social sciences, four in natural sciences, three in humanities, and one in mathematics, plus two in military science for men and two in physical education for women). When Latin joined Greek as an elective, even for the traditional A.B. degree, the university severed another tie with the antebellum past. Tuition was $40 a quarter with out-of-staters paying an additional $33 a quarter or $100 for an academic year of three quarters. Women at the Coordinate College (where room and board were required) paid $110 a quarter with outsiders adding the usual $33 per quarter. Generally costs were low, and unemployment drove many to seek advanced education or training. By the time President Sanford assumed the chancellorship of the University System in 1935, over twenty-five hundred students were jammed into the classrooms and dormitories of the University of Georgia, and two years later enrollment topped three thousand for the first time.

The university was bulging at the seams and costs were increasing steadily, but help did not come immediately. President Franklin D. Roosevelt's New Deal offered relief funds to many segments of the nation's depression-ridden economy, and his Public Works Administration granted loans for college construction, but Governor Eugene Talmadge's bitter opposition to Roosevelt and his program delayed federal assistance. Under heavy pressure from the regents, Talmadge did finally persuade the legislature to put up one million dollars for college construction, but this appropriation was not made until mid-1935, so the real building boom at the University of Georgia did not come until Harmon W. Caldwell took over as president.

Born near La Grange in 1889, Caldwell received his A.B. degree from the university in 1919 and took a law degreee at Harvard in 1924. He taught law at Emory, practiced in Atlanta, and became a professor of law at the University of Georgia in 1929 and dean of the law school in 1933. Two years later he succeeded Sanford as president. Caldwell served from 1935 to 1948, a period when the university, the state, and the nation all made great strides. Among Caldwell's most important tasks was helping to oversee the construction program that Chancellor Sanford had begun, which transformed the campus before World War II.

Fortunately for the university's plans, Governor Talmadge, who failed to unseat Senator Richard B. Russell in 1936, could not run again for the governorship when his term ended early in 1937. The new governor, Eurith D. Rivers (a Young Harris graduate), was pro–New Deal, and the whole university system could finally exploit PWA and other federal funds as well as the million dollars provided by the state in 1935. Chancellor Sanford lobbied skillfully in Washington, and the university furthered its own cause by presenting President Roosevelt with an honorary doctor of laws degree at commencement in 1938. Roosevelt had built a second home, the Little White House, at Warm Springs, and he was delighted to come to Athens and charm another crowd.

The University System received almost $2,500,000 in federal construction grants (not loans). All told before 1940 the system spent $5,656,000 on eighty new buildings. President Caldwell presented the University of Georgia's case effectively, and Chancellor Sanford, who had spent most of his adult life working up the administrative ladder on the Athens campus, cooperated fully. Almost $2,000,000 in state and federal funds went into seventeen new buildings at the university: six scattered dormitories; on the north campus the Science Building (now LeConte Hall for history), the Demonstration School for the College of Education (now Baldwin Hall for political science, anthropology, and sociology), a classroom building for English and foreign languages (now Park Hall), and the Fine Arts Building; on the south campus buildings for agricultural extension, forestry, dairy science, and home economics, and Snelling Hall, a cafeteria. In addition, thorough renovations were carried out in old buildings like

Although the literary societies were no longer the center of university life, many bright young men still honed their intellectual and rhetorical skills at meetings of Phi Kappa and Demosthenian, and the spirited rivalry continued. In 1937 the officers of Phi Kappa went to Warm Springs, Georgia, to initiate Franklin D. Roosevelt into their ancient society. Here the president is surrounded by Phi Kappas, including Registrar Thomas W. Reed (third from left) and Morris B. Abram (fifth from

left). "Uncle Tom" Reed chided the president for his scheme to pack the Supreme Court, but Roosevelt turned aside the criticism with a joke and continued to charm his visitors. Abram, an outstanding student, received his B.A. in 1938 and later won a Rhodes scholarship. A liberal southern lawyer, he successfully challenged Georgia's county-unit voting system before the Supreme Court in 1963. A prominent

attorney in New York and a former president of Brandeis University (1968–1970), Abram also served the nation on numerous commissions and special assignments and spent five years in the air force during World War II. His autobiography, The Day Is Short, *describes the initiation of Roosevelt and the pride of his father, a Jewish immigrant who saw his son already beginning to rise in the new land. (Courtesy of Morris B. Abram.)*

Moore College (which continued to house physics) and New College (which became the new home of the growing School of Pharmacy). A separate grant gave the university eighteen hundred nearby acres which included White Hall, a Victorian mansion now used by the School of Forest Resources as a reception center. And in 1940 Judge Price Gilbert gave $78,000 for a modern infirmary in honor of his son, who had died soon after graduating from the university. The campus changed almost

overnight under the direction of Professor Rudolph H. Driftmier, head of the agricultural engineering department, who supervised the building for the entire University System. All over campus roads and walks were paved and landscaping was systematically carried out, and for many years Oscar Winemiller, "the familiar little man on the horse," struggled to control the trampling and trashing by the student body, which had swelled to almost thirty-seven hundred by 1940.

The great building boom of the late 1930s boosted the university confidently into the new decade of the 1940s. The terrible congestion had been relieved, and steady academic progress continued. Professors like John Donald Wade, Lamar Dodd, and George H. Boyd established national reputations in their specialties. Wade, a native of Marshallville, Georgia, received his A.B. at the university in 1914 and his Ph.D. in literature from Columbia in 1924. He was one of the Nashville Agrarians, who exercised a powerful influence on American literature. After the Second World War he established the *Georgia Review,* a respected literary quarterly. Dodd, a native of Fairburn, studied architecture at Georgia Tech and art with the Art Students League in New York. He came to the university in 1937, and the next year he became head of the Department of Art as he began to establish a reputation as a distinguished painter. During Dodd's forty years as head the number of resident students majoring in art grew from eight to nearly eight hundred. Boyd, also a native of Fairburn, received his A.B. from Emory in 1917 and went on to earn a Sc.D. in medical zoology from Johns Hopkins. While head of the zoology department at the university, he did outstanding research on malaria in birds (closely related to malaria in humans, which plagued the South for centuries). After the war, as dean of the Graduate School, he played a major role in developing research and advanced higher education at the university. Appropriately enough, the Graduate Studies Building was named in his honor in 1972.

Social life at the university remained lively during the 1940s, and athletics flourished. Women were still restricted to intramurals, but men fielded intercollegiate teams in track, cross country, boxing, baseball, basketball, football, and, as long as an ROTC cavalry unit remained on campus, polo. Football remained king. The old rivalry with Georgia Tech—described by one sportswriter as "clean old-fashioned hate"— had resumed in 1926 with Georgia holding the edge for more than a decade. Coach Harry Mehre (a graduate of Notre Dame) turned out a string of strong teams in this period. In 1939 Wallace Butts (Mercer) took over and led the Bulldogs for more than twenty years. A scrappy

bulldog of a man himself, Butts pioneered sophisticated offenses, especially aerial attacks, and sent to the pros a number of high scorers like Frank Sinkwich (winner of the Heisman Trophy in 1942), Charlie Trippi, Zeke Bratkowski, Johnny Rauch, Johnny Carson, Jimmy Orr, and Fran Tarkenton, and also some burly interior linemen like Marion Campbell. Butts won an impressive 61.4 percent of his games. As early as 1941 his Bulldogs won a major bowl game, and the next year, with Sinkwich and Trippi in the same backfield, they laid claim to a national title after defeating UCLA in the Rose Bowl before ninety thousand fans.

Football players were very popular on campus, but some won much greater fame in later years. Louis Wolfson of Jacksonville, Florida, came to Georgia as a highly touted athlete, but a shoulder injury in the Yale game of 1931 ended his gridiron career, and he left school to fashion a spectacular career in the world of high finance. A teammate of Wolfson's, Spurgeon Chandler, was a fine running back who played for the New York Yankees, acquired the nickname "Spud," and became one of the great pitchers in pro baseball. A few years later Forrest "Spec" Towns, another versatile athlete who played end on the football team, won the 110-meter high hurdles, breaking the world record, at the Berlin Olympics in 1936. A month later in a meet in Norway he lowered his time to 13.7 seconds, a record that stood for fourteen years. He came back to Georgia troubled by the rising militarism in Nazi Germany, and in 1944 he returned to that nation as a captain in the U.S. Seventh Army.

But America remained at peace as the decade of the 1940s dawned. The university continued to make slow but steady progress until 1941, when Gene Talmadge became governor again and dealt his alma mater a stunning blow. He intervened in an internal dispute at the university, attacking Walter D. Cocking, a native of Iowa and dean of the College of Education, for favoring racial integration. Cocking denied the charge—a very serious one in those days of strict Jim Crow segregation. Despite the opposition of Sanford and Caldwell, Talmadge pressed the Board of Regents relentlessly. Soon ugly overtones of anti-Semitism and Yankee ha-

In 1944 the Georgia Tech football team, with its navy V-12 trainees, came to Sanford Stadium and trounced Georgia's civilian team. At the halftime the traditional rivalry was forgotten for a few moments as Presi-

dent Harmon W. Caldwell and the movie star Janet Blair encouraged the fans to buy war bonds to help win the only contest that really mattered, the war against the Axis powers. In the center of the next row is Steadman V. Sanford, who had served at the Uni-

versity of Georgia for forty-two years as professor, dean, and president. At this time he was chancellor of the University System.

tred emerged, together with a few wild charges of communism and sexual misconduct. Finally the beleagured regents yielded to the pressure. Ignoring the evidence (or rather the lack of evidence), they dismissed Cocking and several other University System employees. Regent Sandy Beaver tried without success to deter his old friend Talmadge, and in December 1941 the Southern Association of Colleges and Secondary Schools, denouncing Talmadge for "unprecedented and unjustifiable political interference," withdrew the accreditation of the University of Georgia and the other white schools in the University System, effective September 1942.

The Cocking affair became a major issue in the gubernatorial campaign of 1942. Attorney-general Ellis G. Arnall, who had been a student leader at the University of Georgia and had received his LL.B. there in 1931, challenged Talmadge and pledged to remove the University System from political meddling by writing the regents' independence into the state constitution. Arnall defeated Talmadge decisively, and as soon as he became governor in January 1943 he pushed the necessary amendment through the legislature. It provided for a fifteen-person Board of Regents appointed for staggered terms by the governor, who would no longer be an ex-officio member. The Southern Association restored accreditation to the university and

The Georgia Bulldogs play for a dance in 1944. Women greatly outnumbered male students during the war, but social life continued as normally as possible.

the other white schools in the system, and the immediate crisis passed.

Yet serious damage had been done. The most blatant prejudices had swamped the university (which, after all, had been founded by Yankees and had long welcomed Jewish students and contributions). At the very time it was struggling to gain respect and status, it was held up to public censure and ridicule. The hard times between the world wars saw many political and ideological assaults on higher education, and "radicals" sometimes had a rough time at Emory and Mercer as well, but the short accreditation war at the university had been especially damaging.

By this time a far greater war had engulfed the world. This time the Yanks went "over there" in two directions, across the Atlantic and the Pacific oceans. Over three hundred thousand never returned. Once again the University of Georgia went to war, and about two hundred

of her sons gave their lives for the final victory. Already hurt by the accreditation war with Talmadge, enrollment dropped further as many young men were drafted; by 1944 the number of regular students fell below two thousand. Some of the faculty departed for wartime service, among them Professor Rufus H. Snyder, a physicist who contributed to the construction of atomic weapons at Oak Ridge, Tennessee. At the university women students outnumbered regular male students for the first time. Southern ladies to the core, they generally continued to defer to the traditionally dominant men, but by 1944 a few, like Evelyn Lee, editor-in-chief of the *Georgia Agriculturist*, did assume offices formerly held by men.

Colonel K. T. Riggs continued the old ROTC program among the diminished male student body, and the new Civilian Pilot Training Service for 250 men operated in the leased Costa

160

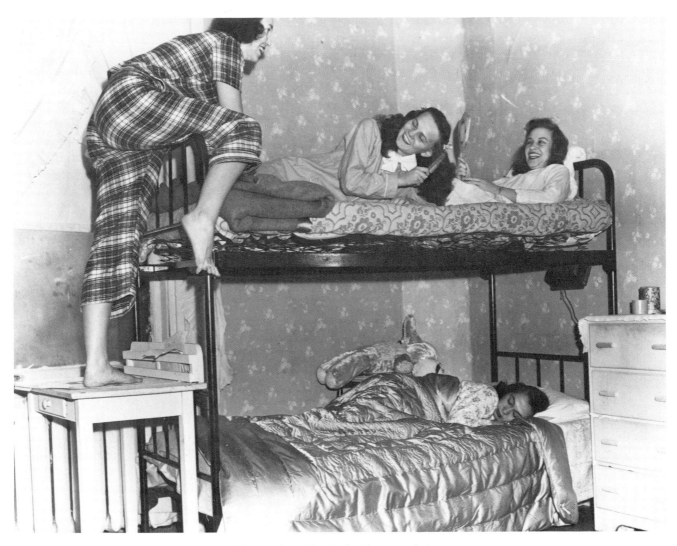

Right after World War II life at the university returned to normal and the Greeks flourished. Here, in 1946, *four Delta Delta Delta sisters settle in for the evening at their sorority house.*

Building on Washington Street. The Army Signal Corps and the Army Specialized Training Program operated much larger programs on campus during the war, but the navy had the greatest impact by placing at the University of Georgia one of its five preflight schools with a steady enrollment of over six thousand men.

The university copied the preflight school's accelerated twelve-month schedule, with increased emphasis on mathematics and the sciences for the duration. As its training program developed, the navy took over many campus facilities, including Baldwin Hall (which became headquarters), Memorial Hall, Woodruff Hall, Snelling Hall, the agronomy barn, and six dormitories, which were given military designations. Old College ("Ranger Barracks") and

Candler Hall ("Yorktown Barracks") were also thoroughly renovated on the inside. The navy also built several new buildings: two long, narrow dormitory-barracks on the south campus, an annex to Memorial Hall, a rear annex to Baldwin Hall as a dining hall, Stegeman Hall with its gymnasium and swimming pool, and a long field house (now Alumni House) to accompany a new track and four new football fields. The navy bore more than half the total cost of all this, and when the war ended the university retained possession of all these campus improvements and additions.

With the coming of peace in 1945 the United States demobilized rapidly. Before the end of the year veterans flooded back into civilian life.

The GI Bill of Rights provided federal funds for veterans to attend the college of their choice for one year plus the time of service in the armed forces up to a maximum of four years. All over the nation veterans went back to school, and college enrollments soared.

The University of Georgia got its full share; by 1948 almost eight thousand students attended classes. More than half were veterans, bringing millions of dollars of federal funds to the bulging university. Much like the Civil War veterans whom Chancellor Lipscomb had described as a "new race of students," these survivors of World War II were generally serious about school. Trying to impose traditional freshman discipline on such men was practically out of the question, and gradually much of the old hazing began to fade away, except in the fraternities. Married veterans set up housekeeping in wooden barracks left over from the preflight program, and these "temporary" structures survived for well over a decade. A shorter-lived trailer village grew up on south campus to help handle married students. By 1950 the tide of veterans began to recede, but many went on to distinguished careers. George Busbee (B.B.A. 1949; LL.B. 1952), governor from 1975 to 1983, and Tom Murphy (LL.B. 1949), longtime Speaker of the Georgia House of Representatives, continued the university's old tradition of dominating state politics. Jack Davis traveled a newer route to prominence by studying art and embarking on a successful career as a commercial artist. Sprinkled in among this host of male veterans were a few former WACs and WAVEs who organized their own League of Women Veterans to go with the men's American Legion post.

At the height of the influx of veterans in 1948 Harmon Caldwell resigned as president of the University of Georgia to become chancellor of the University System. During his thirteen-year administration the school had made considerable progress. The physical plant had been greatly expanded, and in 1946 the School of Veterinary Medicine was reestablished (the eleventh in the nation). For several years it had to operate in borrowed quarters on the south campus, but soon it grew rapidly under the direction of Dean Thomas J. Jones. In 1947 the university took over the night school in Atlanta,

run first by Georgia Tech and then by the University System. Its five thousand students concentrated on courses in commerce and business, and when it became the Atlanta Division of the University of Georgia it mushroomed right along with its host city. Strengthened by its tie with the established university in Athens, it became the independent Georgia State College of Business Administration in 1955 and finally emerged as Georgia State University, joining Tech and Georgia at the forefront of education in the state.

Caldwell made many other academic improvements during his administration. The University of Georgia Press had been established in 1937; under Ralph Stephens, who served as director from 1950 to 1978, it published a growing number of scholarly books. Caldwell allowed much more money for faculty research and publication as the graduate program grew steadily under Dean Boyd. He also shifted more funds to the library, the heart of any university, and in 1937 the university bought the DeRenne library, a large collection of rare books on Georgia. By 1948, despite a thirty-five-thousand-dollar extension, the old Peabody Library could not hold the more than two hundred thousand volumes, which overflowed into several storage annexes in town. A tedious but essential recataloging of the whole collection under the Library of Congress system had begun as well. In 1939 Ilah Dunlap Little's very detailed bequest of four hundred thousand dollars for a new library building presaged better days, but a shortage of additional funds kept Caldwell from constructing it.

Caldwell had worked tirelessly for thirteen years to improve the university, preparing the way for later growth. Building on the foundation laid by Hill and Barrow and reinforced in the brief tenures of Snelling and Sanford, he had brought the university to the very threshold of a new era by the time he moved up to the chancellorship in 1948.

His replacement, Jonathan Clark Rogers, president of North Georgia College at Dahlonega, led the university for only twenty months. As the veterans graduated, enrollment dipped to around six thousand before bottoming out at five thousand two years later. As veterans left so

In the fall of 1942 an enthusiastic crowd of students turned out at the railroad station as the football team left for Memphis and a game against the University of Mississippi. Georgia won 48–13.

did their GI Bill payments from the federal government, and the university's budget remained tight. Even so, Rogers made one major contribution by tying the north and south campuses even more firmly together. He ended the last vestiges of the College of Agriculture's independence by placing the two experiment stations and the Extension Service completely under the control of the new agriculture dean, C. C. Murray, who was, of course, already part of the university's basic administrative structure. As the College of Agriculture came completely into the fold, the medical school in Augusta broke its last tenuous ties to the university in Athens and became the independent Medical College of Georgia. Already accredited and established as a research institution, it prospered on its own, much like Georgia State in Atlanta.

When Rogers retired in September 1950, the regents appointed as his successor Omer Clyde Aderhold, who would guide the university through seventeen years of unprecedented growth and change. The university had begun

as a liberal-arts college, and it had remained so throughout the nineteenth century. For the first half of the twentieth century it had struggled to become a true state university. With Aderhold's inauguration, Georgia began to establish its present position as one of the nation's modern universities, combining teaching, research, and service to meet the needs of an increasingly demanding society.

Born and raised on a farm near Lavonia, Aderhold graduated from the University of Georgia in 1923 with a bachelor of science in agriculture and an M.S. in 1930. In 1938 he received a Ph.D. from Ohio State University. Working his way up at the University of Georgia from an associate professor of rural and vocational education to dean of the College of Education in 1946, he played a major role in improving public schools in Georgia. He was the first president of the university with a background in vocational education and teacher training, and he succeeded in encouraging more specialized and

Home economics was a popular major for women from the time they first matriculated at the university. This 1951 photograph shows students at work in Dawson Hall. Now called the College of Family and Consumer Sci- ences, the program is much expanded and attracts its share of male students as well.

narrowly professional programs without crippling the traditional liberal arts program.

For a few years enrollment remained at about six thousand with a regular faculty of about five hundred. During that period essential new buildings were constructed, mainly with state funds channeled to Athens by Governor Herman Talmadge (LL.B. 1936). The Ilah Dunlap Little bequest was finally combined with state funds to construct a new two-million-dollar library on the north campus where the chancellor's home had stood for over a century. The state alone poured another two million dollars into a center for the School of Veterinary Medicine on the south campus, and two large dormitories, together with various extensions and renovations, soon followed. In 1953 the Kellogg Foundation—surpassing even Peabody's generosity—granted over two million dollars for adult education. The state almost matched this grant, and in 1956 the Georgia Center for Continuing Education was built on the south campus near Lumpkin Street.

As these gleaming new edifices arose, some old satellites fell away. In 1953 the university sold its Coordinate Campus (the old State Normal School) to the U.S. Navy, and, as the Navy Supply Corps School moved in, the freshman and sophomore women eagerly flocked over to the main campus. A few years later the deteriorating main building at old Lucy Cobb Institute on Milledge Avenue was closed as a dormitory, and its students also returned to the main cam-

In 1950 students stroll under the Arch on their way from campus to downtown Athens. The tradition that freshmen were forbidden to walk under the Arch *persisted until the university grew so large that it was no longer* possible *to tell who the freshmen were. (Photograph from the 1950* Pandora.*)*

pus. Still, the university was mindful enough of its antebellum heritage to acquire and renovate an impressive antebellum mansion on Prince Avenue to serve as the president's home.

By this time the Korean War had wound down, but a bitter cold war with the Soviet Union continued. In 1957 Sputnik jarred America's complacency about its scientific and technological superiority. The university's response was the huge Science Center, six large buildings grouped around Conner Hall and costing twelve million dollars (mostly state and university funds). This complex was joined on the south campus in 1964 by a modernistic new pharmacy building costing almost two million

dollars (practically all state funds). Thus all of the sciences moved over to the south campus, leaving the north campus mostly committed to the more traditional social sciences, the humanities, and the law. The construction of the Coliseum for four million dollars (again state money) further emphasized the contemporary spirit of the south campus.

As Georgia's population approached four million, with its cities and industries growing rapidly, the state shed its last ancient shackle, segregation. Like the other deep southern states, Georgia bitterly resisted the Supreme Court's 1954 decision that declared segregated

The typical student's life at the university begins in a small room in one of the larger dormitories. Unpacking is a chore, but there is still time to make new friends and speculate about four years of life at the university. (Photograph by Al Wise, courtesy of the Office of Public Relations.)

schools unconstitutional. But in 1961 the state's determined opposition to integration began to collapse. On January 9 the university, under court order, was forced to admit two black students, Charlayne Hunter and Hamilton Holmes. Governor S. Ernest Vandiver, Jr. (A.B. 1940, LL.B. 1942) threatened to withdraw state funds if the university admitted Hunter and Holmes to classes, but the first two days of integration passed peacefully though tensely.

On the evening of January 11, however, Georgia Tech defeated the Bulldogs in a bitterly contested basketball game in Woodruff Hall. An angry crowd poured out of Woodruff and headed toward Center Myers Hall, Hunter's dormitory. Joined by many nonstudents (including some Klansmen) the crowd swarmed around Myers, smashing windows, chanting "Two, four, six, eight, we don't want to integrate," and waving a banner emblazoned "Nigger Go Home." Dean of Students Joseph A. Williams and Dean of Men William Tate held back the mob until Athens policemen and firemen arrived to end the fracas with tear gas and jets of water. On the next day the administration and the vast majority of the faculty rallied behind the beleaguered black students, and calm returned quickly to the campus. Hunter and Holmes returned to classes on Monday, January 16, and two years later they graduated.

One by one the state's colleges and public schools integrated, however grudgingly. The state of Georgia, with its attention and resources no longer taken up by futile resistance to the law of the land, could now act to modernize its educational system. Under the leadership of Carl E. Sanders (LL.B. 1948) the Board of Regents and the state legislature (now free of the old county-unit system) set out to reform higher education in Georgia and to make the University of Georgia the "capstone institution," the "flagship" of the University System.

On January 9, 1961, Charlayne Hunter and Hamilton Holmes became the first black students to enter the University of Georgia. Here they are surrounded by newsmen as they arrive on campus. The generally peaceful integration of the university was marred by an ugly riot on the evening of January 11, but Holmes and Hunter remained in school and graduated two years later. Both went on to highly successful careers: Holmes as a surgeon and faculty member of the Emory University School of Medicine, and Hunter as an award-winning journalist. (Courtesy of Wide World Photos.)

A turning point came in 1965 when George Simpson, a graduate of the University of North Carolina and an experienced NASA administrator, became chancellor of the fast-growing system. With the approval of the regents he exercised far more sweeping powers than any of his predecessors. Strengthened by huge increases in appropriations for higher education, Simpson worked hard to improve the whole system of thirty-three separate schools, and he showered new funds on the university in Athens.

By this time the university's enrollment was

President Fred C. Davison and his vice-presidents in the new President's Club Garden just south of Old College. Left to right: Davison; Virginia Trotter, vice-president for academic affairs; Dwight Douglas, vice-president for student affairs; Allan W. Barber, vice-president for business and finance; H. Perk Robins, vice-president for development and university relations; and S. Eugene Younts, vice-president for services. Robert C. Anderson, vice-president for research, is not pictured. The low wall just behind these officials bears the names of members of the President's Club, who contributed or pledged ten thousand dollars or more to the university. (Photograph by Walker Montgomery, courtesy of the Office of Public Relations.)

soaring past twelve thousand. President Aderhold in only eighteen months virtually doubled the size of the instructional faculty, to over twelve hundred. Competing in a tight academic market, expanding universities like Georgia finally had to pay solid middle-class salaries to average faculty members and much larger amounts to eminent scholars who would immediately enhance the school's reputation. For the first time Georgia had the money to compete for talented faculty and at the same time to continue a frantic building program.

Exhausted and in poor health, Aderhold retired in 1967. The regents appointed Simpson's thirty-seven-year-old vice-chancellor, Fred C. Davison, as the university's seventeenth president. Born of a New Jersey father and an English mother, Davison grew up in Marietta. After completing his veterinary training in 1952 at the University of Georgia (where he met his future wife, one of the two women in his class), he practiced in Marietta for six years. Then he went to Iowa State University, where in 1963 he received his Ph.D. in pathology and biochemistry. He led a research project for the Atomic Energy Commission before returning to Georgia as dean of the College of Veterinary Medicine in 1964. Like Aderhold, he was trained in a specialized, technical discipline, but, again like Aderhold, he succeeded in advancing the scientific and technical programs now concentrated on the south campus without undermining the traditional liberal arts program on the north

New buildings continue to appear on the campus. In the fall of 1983 the William Tate Student Center was for- *mally dedicated. In the background a covered walkway emerges from the Tate Center and points toward the* *nearby University Bookstore. (Photograph by Walker Montgomery, courtesy of the Office of Public Relations.)*

campus. Under Davison rapid growth continued and even accelerated, and growing pains continued to ripple through the university. By 1970 eighteen thousand students were enrolled, including more than three thousand in the rapidly expanding graduate programs, and the instructional faculty grew to fourteen hundred.

The turbulence of the civil rights and Vietnam eras added to tensions on campus, but the traditional conservatism of the university muted the dissonance. Like the brief anti-integration riot in 1961, the demonstrations later in the 1960s and in the early 1970s served as a safety valve, but even the most radical students held back from the excesses that crippled some other campuses. One of the most significant changes in this period was the university's abandonment of its traditional role as parent away from home. Many of the old rules vanished, and women finally escaped from the old dress and

conduct codes and dormitory restrictions designed for southern ladies of an earlier age. But the university's greatest notoriety in this period may have come during the good-natured madness called streaking when briefly in 1974 old Georgia claimed the national record for the number of students bounding stark naked through the campus.

During the 1970s and early 1980s growth continued, though more slowly after enrollment reached twenty thousand in 1972. Under Davison the building program often took the form of additions to existing structures and complexes. Yet these too were expensive: during the past fifteen years the university has spent over $70 million on such projects. The flourishing Law School acquired new facilities at a cost of $4.5 million; $8.3 million was invested in new quarters for the College of Veterinary Medicine; an annex to the Main Library (which now houses over two million books) cost over $5 million. The Callaway Foundation has contributed generously to the university's botanical garden a few miles south of Athens. On the north campus an academic building named for Harmon Caldwell cost $3.7 million, and the Tate Center, dedicated in the fall of 1983, required well over $6.5 million.

Clearly the state of Georgia was finally pouring generous resources into its main university in Athens, and as a land-grant college the university continued to receive large amounts of direct and indirect federal support as well. The alumni gave so generously to their old school that in 1980 Georgia was recognized as the top-ranked public university in sustained alumni support. Private donations in general increased as a growing number of latter-day George Foster Peabodys gave almost everything imaginable—rare books and documents, oil paintings and other works of art, scholarships and endowments, cold cash, and on one occasion five thousand ampules of frozen bull semen.

The campus was almost swimming in money and resources. The largest amount—over $13 million—was pumped into Sanford Stadium by the independent Athletic Association. Nestling between the north and south campuses, the field was almost surrounded by towering concrete stands seating eighty-two thousand. The football teams that played in Sanford Stadium were equally spectacular. By 1980, when the Bulldogs won their first national championship, Coach Vince Dooley had already compiled a 130–56–6 record over eighteen seasons. Taking over a program that had faltered after Wally Butts retired in 1960, Dooley came to Athens in 1964 from Auburn, where he had earned an M.A. in history while serving as an assistant coach under "Shug" Jordan. "Dooley's Dawgs" took a drubbing in their first game against mighty Alabama but then rolled on to a 6–3–1 season and a bowl victory. In 1965

Georgia again faced Alabama first, but this time they managed a stunning upset victory over "Bear" Bryant's team, which was headed for a national championship. The victories continued to pile up over the years, including a dramatic come-from-behind triumph over Georgia Tech on national television in 1971 and an almost unbelievable last-minute win over Florida toward the end of the undefeated 1980 season. At the end of that season Georgia, led by its spectacular freshman running back, Herschel Walker, defeated Notre Dame in the Sugar Bowl and thus became the national champion.

The next fall a huge influx of freshmen drove enrollment up to almost twenty-four thousand, taxing the facilities and the regular faculty of two thousand. In busy classrooms and laboratories thousands of students worked quietly to prepare themselves for varied careers in the state and the nation while professors directed them, carried out their own research, and reached out to serve the community. Eugene P. Odum (ecology) and Glenn W. Burton (agronomy) gained admission to the National Academy of Sciences, and in 1972 a third member, Norman H. Giles (genetics), moved from Yale to the university. By then the university resembled other state universities much more closely than it did Yale, but this faint hint of the old connection echoed back through two centuries of struggle and progress.

Facing page: Snow flurries are not rare in Athens, but the snow usually melts as soon as it falls. Occasionally, perhaps once a year, snow covers the ground, *and all of Athens stops to enjoy it. The snow is usually gone by the next day. This view of north campus in a light* *coat of snow shows the portico of the Chapel and, in the distance, Old College. (Courtesy of the Office of Public Relations.)*

On December 1, 1934, at the halftime of the Georgia-Tech football game in Atlanta, five distinguished alumni were honored with "G" blankets (the kind football players used on the sidelines). At the far left is George "Kid" Woodruff (class of 1911), a prosperous businessman in Columbus who served for one dollar a year as coach of the football team from 1923 through 1927. On his right is Marion Smith (class of 1903), a prominent Atlanta lawyer who was the son of Governor Hoke Smith. In the center is Sandy Beaver (class of 1903) who played alongside Smith on the football team and later became the head of Riverside Military Academy. To Beaver's right is Alfred O. Halsey (class of 1893), a successful Charleston businessman who was captain of the first football team in 1892 and also starred in baseball. At the far right is Charles H. Herty (class of 1886), adjunct professor of chemistry at the university for eleven years. Herty brought intercollegiate football and basketball to Athens before leaving to begin a distinguished career in industrial chemistry. At this time Woodruff, Smith, and Beaver were also members of the Board of Regents of the University System of Georgia.

Left: Following a tradition that goes back to the very beginning when the university began near the turbulent frontier, the sheriff of Clarke County leads the graduation procession armed with a sword. (Photograph from the 1933 Pandora.)

Below: Repairing the Chapel painting, 1936. This painting of the interior of St. Peter's in Rome by George Cooke measures 17 feet by 23½ feet. It was presented to the university by the Alabama industrialist Daniel Pratt in 1867. After some earlier touching up by Jennie Smith, a teacher at Lucy Cobb Institute, it was repaired again in 1936 by P. H. Baumgarten of the O'Brien Gallery in Chicago, who is shown here on his scaffold. In 1955 the painting was badly damaged by a fire. A local artist, Walter Frobos, and his daughter spent eighteen months restoring the old painting, mounting it on masonite, and framing it in redwood. (Courtesy of Susan B. Tate.)

173

President Franklin Roosevelt spent much time at Warm Springs receiving treatment for polio, but he came to Athens only once. On August 5, 1938, at the summer-school graduation in Sanford Stadium, he was awarded an honorary doctor of laws degree. Here Roosevelt chats with Steadman V. Sanford, chancellor of the University System, and Governor Eurith D. Rivers.

Established in 1903, the pharmacy department struggled along in cramped quarters in the basement of Terrell Hall until 1939, when it took over the top two floors of New College. In the same year Robert C. Wilson, dean for thirty-two years, played an active role at the American Pharmaceutical Association's national meeting in Atlanta. Here he broadcasts an official welcome to the delegates while his wife looks on at the far right. The top row is composed of officials of the organization and prominent local druggists. Under Dean Kenneth Waters, who succeeded Wilson in 1948 and served for twenty-nine years, the School of Pharmacy left the north campus in 1964 and moved into a well-equipped new building on the south campus, where the other scientific and technological specialties are concentrated.

Afternoon tea at Kappa Alpha Theta, 1930s. Concentrated along Milledge Avenue, the sororities built fine new houses and in some cases restored old residences that would otherwise have been demolished. The sororities continued to flourish, and most of them still maintain houses along Milledge Avenue. (Courtesy of Kenneth Kay.)

Above: The only Georgia athlete to gain a gold medal, Forrest "Spec" Towns won the 110-meter high hurdles in the 1936 Berlin Olympics. Towns broke the world record, and a month later he lowered his time to 13.7 seconds, a record that stood for fourteen years. Towns also played football, and after graduating he remained on campus as part of the growing coaching staff. He established a record by coaching the track team from 1938 to 1975 with time off for military service during World War II. (Courtesy of Georgia Sports Information.)

*Above: An ROTC instructor, Major
A. T. Colley, formed the first polo
team at Georgia in 1928, using the
horses in the cavalry unit on campus.
During the 1930s the Georgia cadets
fielded a team of no special distinction
on a field near the modern Coliseum.
With the coming of World War II the
cavalry unit at Georgia was disbanded, and that was the end of polo
in Athens.*

*Left and facing page, below: Wearing
the standard bloomers of the 1930s,
women students participate in gymnastics and track on the south campus as
part of the extensive intramural and
physical education program of the
Women's Athletic Association. The
1933* Pandora *identifies the jumper
as Liddy Rice.*

Above: The university's registrar, "Uncle Tom" Reed, hands out diplomas to proud graduates in Woodruff Hall in the 1930s. Although the student body was growing rapidly, diplomas could still be awarded individually. Some of the more modern degrees were written in English, but the traditional liberal arts degrees were still written in Latin. (Courtesy of Kenneth Kay.)

Facing page, above: In the late 1930s newer fields like psychology began to attract many majors. Here Saidee Hodgson of Athens and Robert W. Schnautz of Rye, New York, one of a growing number of northern students, collapse soon after completing an experiment in which they stayed awake for a hundred hours to determine the effect of sleeplessness on mind and body.

Facing page, below: By the 1930s the university was growing steadily and making a serious effort to maintain an attractive campus. The grounds foreman, Oscar Winemiller, waged a relentless struggle to keep the students from trampling and littering his domain. His remedy for illegally parked autos was direct and effective—he let the air out of the tires. Known to students as "the little man on the horse," Winemiller roamed the campus, one of the pioneers in the beautification of a campus that had received very little attention for over a century. (Photograph from the 1937 Pandora.)

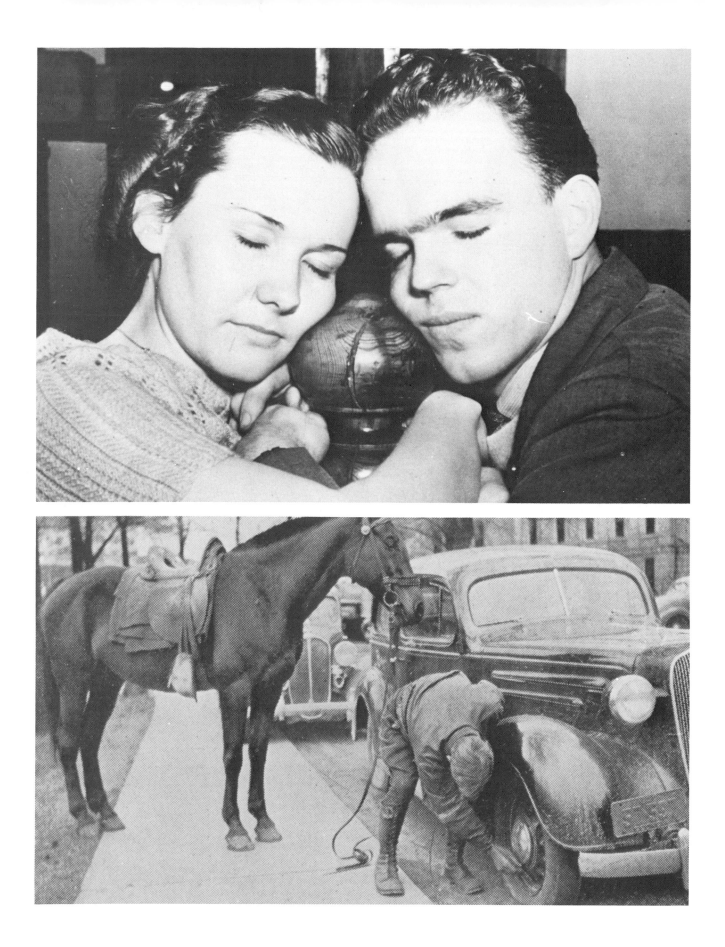

179

Above: During the depression federal funds, especially from the Public Works Administration, poured into campus building projects. Here early in 1938 the foundations of Baldwin Hall are dug on the edge of the old university graveyard on the north campus. The building was completed the same year as the Demonstration School for the College of Education. During World War II the navy added a rear annex as a dining hall. Baldwin Hall housed the biological sciences for years and then the main offices of the College of Education from 1962 to 1971. Now it houses sociology, political science, and anthropology. In the distance from left to right can be seen Milledge Hall, Conner Hall, and Memorial Hall, and on the right behind the tool shed stands LeConte Hall, another PWA building that had just been finished for the biological sciences. LeConte now houses the history department. (Courtesy of the Georgia Department of Archives and History.)

Facing page, above: Federal funds poured onto south campus to expand operations like home economics as the building boom of the 1930s continued. Seventeen new buildings were constructed during this period. Completed in 1939—and still standing—these home management houses (four in all) served as residences for home ec majors who had to live there for a quarter in fulfillment of a laboratory requirement. The buildings were later used for administrative offices. (Courtesy of the Georgia Department of Archives and History.)

Facing page, below: In the summer of 1939 workers put the final touches on Rutherford Hall, a new dormitory for women on the growing south campus. (Courtesy of the Georgia Department of Archives and History.)

The tennis team of 1941 poses with LeConte Hall in the background. Dan Magill, who coached the tennis team from 1955–1995, is second from the left. Late in the nineteenth century students played tennis on four dirt courts between Phi Kappa Hall and Broad Street. By the 1940s, the courts shown here had been built on Baldwin Street on the site of the present Psychology-Journalism Complex. The tennis teams later played at the Dan Magill Tennis Complex, which has also been one of the regular host sites of the NCAA tournament.

New members of Sphinx, the most prestigious nonacademic society for male undergraduates, lampoon Governor Eugene Talmadge (LL.B. 1908). Just beginning a second term as governor in 1941, Talmadge denounced Dean Walter D. Cocking of the College of Education as an integrationist and forced the regents to dismiss him and several other employees of the University System. The Southern Association of Colleges and Secondary Schools denounced this political interference and in December 1941, just before Pearl Harbor, withdrew accreditation from all of the white schools in the University System. Faced with the prospect of receiving worthless degrees, Georgia students denounced Governor Talmadge in a series of demonstrations and rallied behind Attorney General Ellis G. Arnall (LL.B. 1931). In the heated gubernatorial campaign of 1942 Arnall won decisively, and the Georgia schools were soon reaccredited. (Photograph from the 1942 Pandora.)

Above: The 1942 Georgia backfield goes through its paces. From left to right: Frank Sinkwich (All-American and Georgia's first Heisman Trophy winner), Charley Trippi (soon to be All-American), Dick McPhee, and Lamar Davis. McPhee was a solid player and Davis was an outstanding runner, but Sinkwich and Trippi were superstars, the kind that usually came along once in a generation. Sinkwich and Trippi both played professional football, after which they pursued business careers in Athens. (Courtesy of Georgia Sports Information.)

Right: Frank Sinkwich, an All-American and the winner of the Heisman Trophy, was the center of attention when Georgia came to California to play UCLA in the Rose Bowl on January 1, 1943. A 9–0 victory before ninety thousand spectators ended a season marred only by a loss to Auburn.

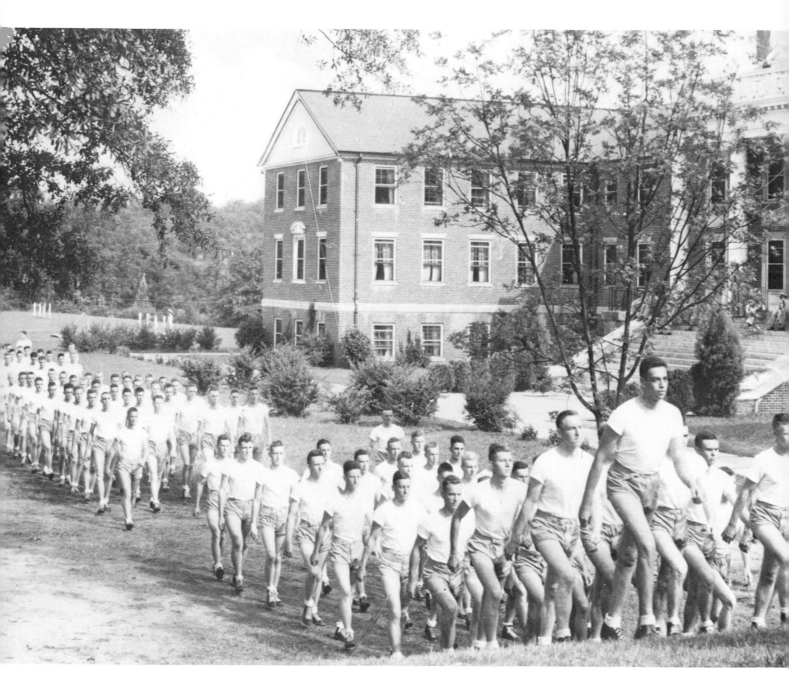

During World War II the U.S. Navy's preflight program, enrolling over six thousand men, changed the face of the university. The photograph above (courtesy of the Georgia Historical Society) shows a detachment of trainees marching past Rutherford Hall on their way to the athletic fields. In the photograph at the bottom of the facing page the trainees stand formation in the amphitheater (now the site of the Graduate Studies Building) and receive their instructions for the day. In the background is Soule Hall, the first women's dormitory.

Left: On November 11, 1941, the university ROTC troops joined the traditional Armistice Day parade in Athens celebrating victory in World War I. World War II had been raging for two years in Europe, and less than a month later the Japanese attack on Pearl Harbor brought America into the war. These part-time soldiers were among the first university men to fight. Almost two hundred University of Georgia men were killed during World War II. (Photograph from the 1942 Pandora.)

Above: America's entry into World War II brought great changes to the campus, but some tradition persisted. On March 5, 1943, the Chi Omegas held their formal dance as usual. Here Karen Smith, Mary Sue Martin, Dorothy Ann Wellman, and their dates enter the Georgian Hotel at the beginning of the party. (Photograph from the 1943 Pandora.)

Facing page, above: Led by Charley Trippi, who returned from the army in the middle of the season, the 1945 football team won eight of its ten games and traveled to Houston to defeat Tulsa in the Oil Bowl. Here the visitors pose for photographers before the game: (left to right) in the white coat, quarterback Johnny Rauch, who became an All-American; in the black coat, Coach Wally Butts; behind the driver of the motorcycle, Charley Trippi. In the background just beyond the white sombrero, in an open-necked shirt, is Carl Sanders, who became governor of Georgia in 1963.

Facing page, below: After World War II many veterans came to the university. One was Jack Davis, who studied in Lamar Dodd's art department and contributed to a short-lived underground campus magazine called the Bull Sheet. This Davis cartoon parodies a favorite campus activity, the river party. Davis entered the highly competitive world of commercial art and became a major contributor to Mad magazine.

Facing page, above: A rather reserved man, President Harmon W. Caldwell was still reasonably accessible to the student body, which numbered twenty-three hundred in 1945. Here he is interviewed by journalism students in his office. (Photograph from 1945 Bulletin.)

Facing page, below: By 1948 the university was moving out into the state in many different fields, including archaeological excavations of Indian sites. Here university personnel pose around a digging site in the Allatoona basin. Kneeling, left to right, are E. Merton Coulter, historian; Joseph H. Mahan, archaeologist; Arthur R. Kelley, the archaeologist who excavated so many sites in Georgia that he became known as "Digger"; and W. H. Sears, archaeological supervisor. Standing, left to right, are George H. Boyd, dean of the Graduate School; Dean of Men William Tate; Dean of Faculties Alvin B. Biscoe; Treasurer J. D. Bolton; and President Jonathan C. Rogers. (Courtesy of Susan B. Tate.)

Above: The sixteen members of the Red and Black's staff gather in 1943 to plan future issues. Before the war ended, the number of women working on publications and other extracurricular activities would increase.

Facing page: A graduate of Hampden-Sydney College in Virginia, Willis H. Bocock came to the University of Georgia as professor of ancient languages in 1889 and taught Greek for fifty-six years. He was dean of the Graduate School for almost two decades, and later he served for many years as dean of the faculty. He retired in 1945 when the university put into effect its first retirement system and died two years later at the age of eighty-two. Here late in his career he examines his newspaper and documents collection, which he used to teach a course in international relations.

Above: The Demosthenian Literary Society, though much diminished in size and importance, is still active on campus. Here in 1944 a speaker delivers his message, just as Demosthenians have done since the society began in 1803.

Above: Taking a break at the Co-op in 1950. During the 1930s the first floor of New College held the book store on one side and the Co-op on the other. Operated for years by Compton O. "Fat" Baker, the Co-op remained there until the early 1950s. The conversation was free and food was inexpensive: a cheese sandwich cost fifteen cents and for a nickel more you got a slice of ham. (Photograph from the 1950 Pandora.)

Right: Fraternities and sororities compete for the best homecoming decorations during the football season. Here the Zeta Tau Alpha sorority displays an atomic age setting in the 1950s. (Photograph from the 1951 Pandora.)

Two drum majorettes get ready for a performance of the university marching band in the 1950s. (Photograph from the 1950 Pandora.*)*

Above: In 1951 a visiting expert lectures Georgia students on the fine points of pool, still a man's game in the 1950s. (Photograph from the Annual Report, 1951–1952.)

Right: Women from the Atlanta Division of the University of Georgia ride in a parade down Peachtree Street, 1952. Originally established by Georgia Tech and then continued by the University System, the night school in Atlanta had over five thousand students, mostly part time. In 1947 it was taken over by the university and renamed the Atlanta Division of the University of Georgia. Growing with its host city, it became the independent Georgia State College of Business Administration in the 1950s. Now a university, it has joined Georgia and Georgia Tech at the forefront of higher education in the state.

194

Left: In 1939 Ilah Dunlap Little left four hundred thousand dollars for the construction of a new library at the university, but work was not begun because funds were not available to cover the rest of the nearly $2 million cost. Finally in 1950 the additional funds came from the state, the old President's House was demolished, and work began on that site. By the spring of 1952, when this photograph was taken, the building was nearing completion. In the fall of 1953 the school's nearly three hundred thousand volumes were moved in, and the building was opened. (Photograph from the Annual Report, 1951–1952.)

Above: Preparing to fire a salvo, a physical education class practices near the Women's Physical Education Building on south campus. The sports uniform for the 1950s was briefer and trimmer, but another decade would pass before such costumes were permissible on the rest of the campus.

195

Above: In the 1950s women students still caught rides to and from classes. Here in the 1950s a group waits in the rain on Lumpkin Street in front of the Chi Phi and Kappa Alpha houses. (Photograph from the 1958 Pandora.)

Right: Beauty contests were important events in the 1950s. Excited contestants in the Miss Pandora competition are shown waiting for a decision. (Photograph from the 1958 Pandora.)

Facing page, above: One of the last vestiges of hazing was the shirttail parade for male freshmen in the fall. Not many years after this exuberant crowd turned out in 1958, the university grew too large for such traditions.

Facing page, below: The university had not yet entered its period of explosive growth, but registration for classes was still an ordeal. Here students stand patiently in line in Woodruff Hall in the 1950s. (Photograph from the 1958 Pandora.)

Facing page, above: A cliffhanger in Sanford Stadium, 1959. With less than a minute left and Auburn winning 13–7, Georgia was only thirteen yards away from a touchdown. Quarterback Francis Asbury Tarkenton (10) hastily made up a play in the huddle, then rolled to his right and fired a perfect strike to the left side of the field to end Bill Herron (81), shown here cradling the ball as he crosses the goal line. With Tarkenton holding, Durward Pennington kicked the winning extra point, and Georgia won the conference championship. Later that year, Georgia defeated Missouri in the Orange Bowl.

Facing page, below: Organized in 1927, the Dolphin Club put on a water pageant every spring in the Women's Physical Education Building. Here in 1959 the women prepare to begin their performance. On the far left of the back row is Karol Ann Kahns, who would go on to become athletic director for women at the University of Illinois.

Above: Robert Frost came south every winter and visited his old friend Hugh Hodgson, head of the music department from 1928 until his retirement in 1960. While in Athens Frost always delivered a lecture in the Chapel or, as the audiences grew over the years, in the Fine Arts Auditorium. Hodgson was an accomplished pianist, organist, and composer. Here Hodgson, Frost, and President O. C. Aderhold pose on campus in 1957. (Photograph from the 1957 Pandora.)

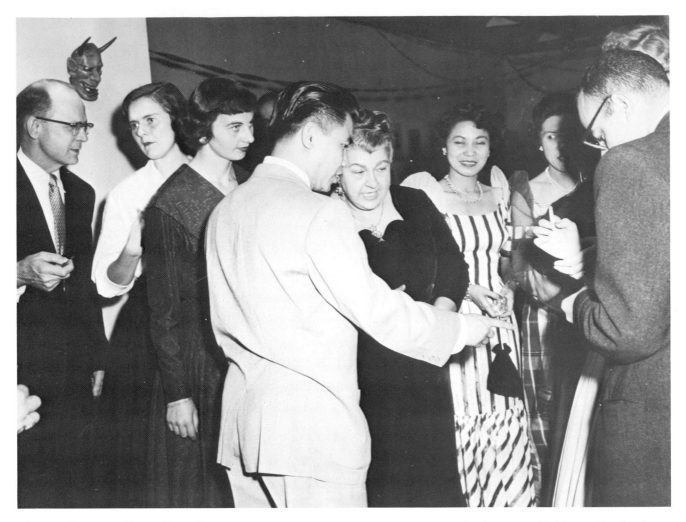

Above: Edith L. Stallings, dean of women from 1948 to 1963, greets foreign students at a reception in the 1950s. A handful of students from other lands were on campus in the 1930s, and by the 1950s they were a familiar sight in Athens. A few years after Dean Stallings retired, the university yielded to mounting protests by women students and abolished the rigid rules that had greatly restricted their activities ever since they first enrolled in 1918. The offices of dean of men and dean of women were combined into the office of dean of students. (Courtesy of the Office of Public Relations.)

Facing page: E. Merton Coulter lectures on American history in a classroom in the Academic Building in the 1950s. Coulter arrived on the campus in 1919 and was one of the first faculty members to gain a national reputation for research and publication. Soon after he retired in 1958, the history department moved to LeConte Hall. Coulter moved to an office in the back of Phi Kappa Hall and continued to publish works on southern history. In 1974 he retired from the editorship of the Georgia Historical Quarterly *after fifty years in that position, but he continued to work until his death in 1981. (Courtesy of the Office of Public Relations.)*

In the fall of *1959* a crowd packs Sanford Stadium and cars fill every available space on the campus. In the foreground to the left the Chemistry Building nears completion, and the Biological Sciences Building begins to rise above its foundations. These two structures were the largest within the new six-building Science Center. Beyond the stadium stands Memorial Hall and behind it Woodruff Hall, which would soon be demolished. The new Ilah Dunlap Little Memorial Library dominates north campus, and beyond the north campus lies downtown Athens.

Facing page, above: The ideal quarter-back for Coach Wally Butts's passing game, Fran Tarkenton won All-American honors on a mediocre team in 1960. Moving on to professional football, he outpassed quarterbacks with stronger arms and set a number of records over eighteen seasons, including most passes thrown (6,467) and most passes completed (3,686). He continued to scramble, and somehow stayed healthy enough to play in 230 games before retiring in 1978. Tarkenton took time from his successful business and television careers to head the university's Bicentennial Capital Campaign in the early 1980s. (Photograph from the 1960 Pandora.)

Facing page, below: The marching band takes a break along the sidelines at Sanford Field early in the 1960s. (Photograph from the Pandora.)

Above: Although he acquired great power and responsibility in Washington, Senator Richard B. Russell, Jr., visited his alma mater frequently. Here in the early 1960s he participates in a television program with students. To the far right on the panel is Tom Johnson, who received his degree in journalism in 1964. Johnson became publisher of the influential Los Angeles Times in 1980 and later moved on to oversee all of CNN's news operations. (Courtesy of the Richard B. Russell Memorial Library, University of Georgia.)

Phi Mu sisters greet rushees in the late 1960s. Sororities have always been the center of the university's social life for many young women. Finding—and being invited to pledge—the right sorority is often a matter of utmost importance. The Greek system weakened a bit in the early 1970s but later regained its popularity and influence. By the late 1990s a total of nearly fifty social sororities and fraternities were present on campus.

Over the years the traditional senior parade continued. By the late 1960s there were too many seniors, so the custom was discontinued. The parade was lively to the end. (Courtesy of the Georgia Alumni Society.)

The Science Center, mid-1960s. Before the bridge linking north and south campus was finished in 1963, students crossing from one side of the campus to the other had to walk down into the ravine and climb back up a steep set of stairs. Only a brand-new freshman would schedule classes for consecutive periods on opposite sides of campus: there were only ten minutes between classes, but the hike took at least twenty. Now, with fifteen minutes between classes and an efficient bus service, most students manage to get to class on time. (Courtesy of the Office of Public Relations.)

Above: David McCord Wright teaches an economics class in the auditorium of the Commerce-Journalism Building, probably in the early 1960s. Large classes like this one were less common then than now. (Photograph by John Stephens, courtesy of the Office of Public Relations.)

Left: The Phi Kappas in 1968. The dwindling membership of the Phi Kappa Literary Society rallies in the old meeting room on the second floor of Phi Kappa Hall. Women had finally been accepted into regular membership. A few years later the Phi Kappas faded away, but the society has since been revived. (Photograph from the 1968 Pandora.)

Change of classes on a cloudy day, mid-1960s. In the 1950s saddle oxfords were standard for women students, but in the sixties they were worn only when it looked like rain. (Courtesy of the Office of Public Relations.)

Right: Comfortably settled into the new Coliseum by the late 1960s, Georgia played a full schedule in a modern facility. Here center Bob Lienhard puts up a shot against Kentucky. (Photograph by Al Wise, courtesy of the Office of Public Relations.)

Below: The Coliseum, completed in 1964, is home to the basketball and gymnastic teams and to athletic department offices. The arena floor can also accommodate exhibitions and concerts. In 1996 it was named Stegeman Coliseum in continuing memory of legendary coach Herman James Stegeman, whose name had adorned the old Stegeman Hall gymnasium until it was demolished in 1995. (Courtesy of the Office of Public Relations.)

Facing page, below: Another beautiful football weekend in Athens begins, and out charges the 1968 football team led by cheerleaders and back Bruce Kemp (30), linebacker Ronnie Huggins (43) and All-American lineman Steve Greer (60). The new upper tier has added thousands of new seats, and the noise level is raised considerably by the Redcoat Band. (Photograph from the 1969 Pandora.)

Above: Young Vince Dooley came to Georgia in 1964 to rebuild the faltering football program, and his first game was against "Bear" Bryant's mighty Crimson Tide. Alabama overwhelmed Georgia 31–3 and rolled on to win the national championship. Dooley regrouped his team and compiled a 7–3–1 record, closing out with identical 7–0 wins over Georgia Tech and over Texas Tech in the Sun Bowl. The following year, before a capacity crowd at Sanford Stadium and a national television audience, Dooley faced the Bear again, but this time Georgia pulled a stunning 18–17 upset. This photograph shows the Georgia players carrying Dooley to center field to receive Bryant's congratulations. (Courtesy of Billy Downs, Atlanta Journal and Constitution.)

During the Vietnam era a series of demonstrations swept through American campuses. Georgia's traditional conservatism muted the dissonance, and the university's demonstrations were peaceful. Here, after the Kent State shootings in the spring of 1970, demonstrators rally at the Academic Building. (Photographs by Walker Montgomery, courtesy of the Office of Public Relations.)

Dean Tate had played a major role in quieting the integration riot on campus in 1961, and during the demonstrations of the late 1960s and early 1970s he again exercised a restraining and moderating influence in tense times. At the time of the killings at Kent State University he donned some love beads and sat quietly among a crowd of student demonstrators.

Above: Under Coach Vince Dooley Georgia football teams compiled an outstanding record, but a couple of seasons were only mediocre and occasionally the worst catastrophe of all occurred—the Bulldogs fell to Georgia Tech. Here two cheerleaders suffer helplessly in 1970 at Sanford Stadium as the Yellow Jackets fashion a convincing 17—7 win on their way to the Sun Bowl. (Photograph from the 1972 Pandora.)

216

Although officially integrated in 1961, the university did not begin to use black athletes for almost a decade. Ronnie Hogue, the first black to play a major sport for Georgia, starred on the basketball team from 1970 to 1973. Horace King was an outstanding running back on the football team from 1972 to 1974, and by then black athletes began to make a major contribution to the sports program. (Courtesy of Georgia Sports Information.)

Facing page, below: Restoring Conner Hall, early 1970s. The first university building on the south campus, Conner Hall had served agriculture for six decades before it was completely demolished on the inside and then rebuilt for greater efficiency and economy. The old three-story staircase was replaced by elevators, and a new central heating and cooling system was installed. During construction the outside brick walls were shored up by steel girders and then restored with little change beyond the addition of modern tinted windows. The work was completed in the spring of 1974. Conner Hall continues to function as the headquarters of the College of Agriculture. (Courtesy of John Toon.)

Above: The library, completed in 1953, was soon bulging at the seams despite the expansion of separate law and science libraries. In 1974 an annex was completed to house the overflow of more than two million volumes in the university's stacks. Towering over the Main Library and dwarfing LeConte Hall in the background, it matches some of the huge structures on the newer south campus. (Courtesy of the Georgia Alumni Society.)

Facing page: After a lifetime of public service, Senator Richard B. Russell, Jr., was buried at his home town of Russell, near Winder. His papers, books, and memorabilia came to the University of Georgia, his alma mater. On June 22, 1974, the Richard B. Russell Memorial Library was officially dedicated and installed in the new annex to the Main Library. Here his sister Mary Russell Green cuts the official ribbon while President Fred C. Davison, Senator Henry Jackson of Washington, Senator Herman E. Talmadge of Georgia, and Governor Jimmy Carter applaud. (Courtesy of the Richard B. Russell Memorial Library, University of Georgia.)

Right: In the 1970s the Pamoja Singers established a strong tradition at the university. They presented an annual concert in the spring and also toured the state. Other groups that recognize and encourage cultural contributions by black students have emerged over the years, including the Black Theatrical Ensemble, the Pamoja Dance Company, and the Abeneefoo Kuo Honor Society. (Photograph from the 1978 Pandora.*)*

Facing page, below: A huge crowd at the October 1977 home game against Kentucky gave a rousing welcome to Prince Charles, heir to the British throne. Escorted by President Fred C. Davison and surrounded by a sea of Redcoats, the prince chatted with two majorettes and the rival coaches, accepted a few souvenirs, and then departed at the end of the third quarter. (Courtesy of John Toon.)

Above: By the 1950s the student body had grown so large that June graduation was shifted from Woodruff Hall to Sanford Stadium in good weather. More and more advanced degrees were awarded each year. Here three brand-new doctors of philosophy savor their hard-won degrees in the 1970s. (Photograph from the Pandora.)

Facing page, above: The Zeta Tau Alphas get ready for a recent homecoming parade through town. (Photograph from the Pandora.)

Facing page, below: The university's twenty-four-inch telescope is used primarily for studies of binary and variable stars. Here it is being operated by J. Scott Shaw and E. G. Reuning of the physics department. (Photograph by Walker Montgomery, courtesy of the Office of Public Relations.)

Above: Georgia's generally mild climate allows professors to take their classes outside occasionally. Here a class discussion takes place in front of the Chapel with New College in the background. (Photograph by Walker Montgomery, courtesy of the Office of Public Relations.)

Facing page, above: In 1977 Waddel Hall (originally Philosophical Hall) was thoroughly renovated and renamed the Rusk Center. Here at the dedication ceremonies Governor George Busbee (class of 1949) speaks from the rostrum in front of the building. Just to the right of the flag is Dean Rusk; on his left is Ladybird Johnson. A native of northern Georgia, Rusk served as secretary of state under Presidents Kennedy and Johnson. In 1970 he became Samuel Sibley Professor of International Law at the University of Georgia and built up the program in international and comparative law. (Photograph by Walker Montgomery, courtesy of the Georgia Alumni Society.)

Facing page, below: Though not one of the major women's sports that began to receive strong support from the athletic department in the mid-1970s, rugby attracted a number of players and progressed well as one of the older club sports for women. (Photograph from the 1978 Pandora.)

Above: While governor of Georgia Jimmy Carter had commissioned six University of Georgia history professors to write a new history of Georgia. By the time the volume was published in 1977 by the University of Georgia Press, Carter was president of the United States. In March 1978 the university sent a delegation of the authors and two university officials to the White House to present a copy of the new book to President Carter. From left to right: Charles E. Wynes; Phinizy Spalding; Numan V. Bartley; F. N. Boney; President Carter; Kenneth Coleman; Ralph H. Stephens, then director of the University of Georgia Press; Fred C. Davison, president of the university; and William F. Holmes. (Courtesy of the White House.)

Right: In 1978 as the Georgia Power Company prepared to construct Wallace Dam to create Lake Oconee in central Georgia, the anthropology department carried out extensive excavations of Indian and white settlement areas. Here students work at the site of the Curtwright Mill, a textile factory that began operations with the latest in machines and technology in the 1840s. (Photograph by Walker Montgomery, courtesy of the Georgia Alumni Society.)

Below: Among the distinguished law school alumni present for Law Day on April 28, 1979, with Dean J. Ralph Beaird (far right) were three former governors of Georgia. From left to right: S. Ernest Vandiver, Jr. (A.B. 1940, LL.B. 1942), Ellis G. Arnall (LL.B. 1931), and Carl E. Sanders (LL.B. 1948). Collectively they symbolize the overwhelming influence university alumni have exercised in state government in modern times. (Photograph by Walker Montgomery, courtesy of the Georgia Alumni Society.)

Above: Confederate flags wave proudly as fans cheer on the Georgia Bulldogs in the 1960s. By the 1970s Confederate themes were disappearing from Sanford Stadium as black players appeared in greater and greater numbers. (Photograph from the Pandora.)

Right: Even as everyday clothing became more and more casual, the old-fashioned beauty pageant continued. Here Lisa Carter is crowned Miss University of Georgia in 1979. (Photograph from the 1979 Pandora.)

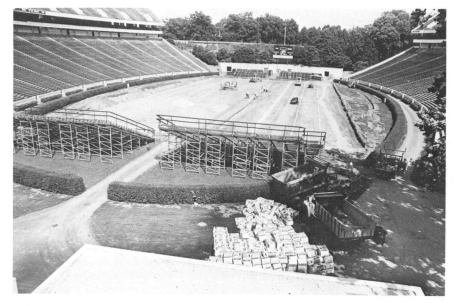

Right: Workers strip away the old surface of the football field and prepare to returf with a new natural grass with improved drainage and watering systems in 1980. (Courtesy of John Toon.)

Facing page, below: The fiercest of all football fans gathered on the railroad embankment just beyond East Campus Drive where the open south end of Sanford Stadium offered an almost unobstructed and completely free view. Though their outside loyalties were as varied as the banners they waved— here the Confederacy, the United States, South Korea, and Omega Tau Alpha—they were united in their loyalty to the Dogs, and they could be harsh to partisans of other teams who strayed too close to their citadel. Here they rise as one to salute their conquering heroes at the end of another home victory late in the 1970s. (Photograph from the Pandora.*)*

Above: In 1981 Sanford Stadium was expanded at the far end to seat a total of 82,000 spectators, and in the summer of 1982 lights were installed so that a national television audience could watch Georgia, national champion for the 1980 season, play Clemson, national champion for the 1981 season. The two powerhouses met be-

tween the hedges and, for the first time since the 1950s, under the lights in Sanford Stadium. Georgia won and rolled on through the season undefeated, but the Bulldogs lost in the Sugar Bowl to Penn State, national champion for the 1982 season. Under Coach Vince Dooley Georgia had become a perennial national powerhouse with a home stadium among the best in the land. (Photograph by Walker Montgomery, courtesy of the Office of Public Relations.)

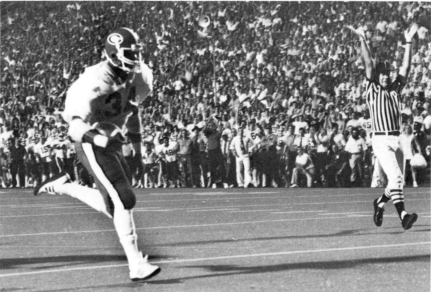

Facing page: Herschel Walker did not start in Georgia's first game of the 1980 season, against Tennessee in Knoxville. Tennessee took an early 15–0 lead. In the third quarter Georgia got a safety and soon had the ball with a first down on Tennessee's sixteen-yard line. Taking a pitchout from quarterback Buck Belue, Walker raced through the line and left several Tennessee players sprawling as he scored his first collegiate touchdown. In the fourth quarter Walker used his unique combination of speed and power to score again, this time from nine yards out. Georgia won 16–15, and Walker and the Bulldogs began their incredible journey, which ended with a Sugar Bowl victory and a national championship. (Courtesy of Perry McIntyre, Jr., Georgia Bulldog Magazine.)

Below: On New Year's Day, 1981, undefeated Georgia squared off in the Sugar Bowl against a powerful Notre Dame team which had won nine, lost one, and tied one. After the teams traded field goals, Notre Dame began to falter, and twice Herschel Walker carried the ball over. Here center Joe Happe prepares to snap the ball to quarterback Buck Belue, who will hand off to the waiting number 34. Walker sailed over the big Irish line for a touchdown and minutes later raced around end for another. Notre Dame could not catch up, and the Bulldogs finally had their glory and their first national championship. (Courtesy of Perry McIntyre, Jr., Georgia Bulldog Magazine.)

Right: By 1974 the university fielded intercollegiate women's teams in basketball, golf, track, swimming, tennis, gymnastics, and volleyball. Led by Kodak All-American Janet Harris, the basketball team made the final four in the NCAA tournament of 1983. Here Harris shoots against Southern California. (Courtesy of Karekin Goekjian.)

Facing page, above: In the 1960s George Handler teaches a class of 317 students in the auditorium of the Chemistry Building. On the wall hangs a portrait of Charles H. Herty, class of 1886, the great industrial chemist and father of Georgia football. (Photograph from the Pandora.)

Facing page, below: Three All-American track men work out in the spring of 1981. From left to right, Herschel Walker, Paul Johnson, and Mel Lattany. (Photograph from the Pandora.)

Left: Completed in 1981, Harmon W. Caldwell Hall rises above the north campus. It is named for the man who served as dean of the law school (1933–1935), president of the university (1935–1948), and chancellor of the University System (1948–1964). The departments of Environmental Design, Historic Preservation, and Landscape Architecture are located there, along with general classroom space. In the foreground is Joe E. Brown Hall, once a dormitory, later home to the comparative literature and Germanic and Slavic languages departments. To the right is Robert Preston Brooks Hall, home of the Terry College of Business Administration. (Photograph by Walker Montgomery, courtesy of the Office of Public Relations.)

Facing page, below: Charlayne Hunter-Gault, whose enrollment helped to end segregation at Georgia in 1961, chats with star Bulldog running back Herschel Walker in November 1981 during one of Hunter-Gault's many visits to the campus over the years. Soon Walker would become famous in his profession too. (Photograph by Walker Montgomery, courtesy of the Office of Public Relations.)

Above: Demonstrations have always been relatively restrained at Georgia, even in the Vietnam era, and by the 1980s a calmer mood had settled over campuses all over the nation. In 1981 graduate students, demonstrating against a new policy that raised their expenses, cross the Sanford Stadium bridge in good order. (Courtesy of John Toon.)

235

236

Left: A native of Athens, Terri Moody was one of the first outstanding intercollegiate athletes to emerge as the university accelerated its women's athletic program in the mid-1970s. Before Moody graduated in 1981 she won recognition as an All-American golfer. (Photograph from the 1981 Pandora.)

Below: Georgia players Bill Rodgers (serving) and John Mangan battle their way to the semifinals of the NCAA doubles competition in 1981. The match was played in Henry F. Feild Stadium, which, since opening in 1977, has frequently been the NCAA tournament's host site. The stadium is part of a still-growing complex named after very successful Coach Dan Magill that boasts indoor and outdoor courts, seating for almost 6,000, and the Collegiate Tennis Hall of Fame. (Courtesy of Georgia Sports Information.)

Facing page: A superb athlete and a master of the spectacular dunk shot, Dominique Wilkins led the Georgia basketball team for three years. He left school at the end of his junior year in 1982 to play professional basketball with the Atlanta Hawks. In 1983 Coach Hugh Durham's well-balanced team won the Southeastern Conference and went all the way to the semifinals— the "final four"—of the NCAA tournament before losing to North Carolina State, the eventual champion. (Courtesy of Georgia Sports Information.)

Facing page, above: A combo entertains a festive crowd outside the Kappa Alpha house on a big party weekend. (Photograph from the 1983 Pandora.)

Facing page, below: By 1983 blacks composed roughly 5 percent of the student population. Although in many ways blacks and whites mingled smoothly, frictions sometimes developed and periodically blacks protested the university's policies and procedures. Here in the spring of 1983 Roosevelt Stripling, vice-president of the Black Student Union, rallies black students on the Memorial Hall Plaza, the main campus site for student speeches and gatherings. In the background is the Psychology-Journalism Complex. (Courtesy of William B. Winburn.)

Above: Miriam Dingle, Miss Black University of Georgia, 1981, takes her place in the winner's car as a photographer fires away and the homecoming parade prepares to wind its way through town. (Photograph from the 1982 Pandora.)

In the early 1800s President Josiah Meigs emphasized science and mathematics, but over time this early stress faded considerably. With the coming of the twentieth century and Conner Hall and the sprawling south campus and the Science Center after World War II, the sciences moved to the fore again. Recently more women have gone into the laboratories in areas like pharmacy, veterinary medicine, and chemistry. (Photograph from the Pandora.)

Eugene P. Odum came to the University of Georgia in 1940 as an instructor in zoology. He helped establish the Marine Institute on Sapelo Island in 1954, and in 1961 he founded the university's Institute of Ecology, now housed in a modern, well-equipped building on south campus. In 1970 he was elected to the National Academy of Science, and since then he has continued to receive worldwide recognition for his work. He has developed a comprehensive ecology program at the university and has written a basic textbook used all over the world. Here Odum, second from left, works with two graduate students and a visiting professor from mainland China at the Horseshoe Bend research site near the south campus. As usual, his main laboratory is the field. (Photograph by Walker Montgomery, courtesy of the Office of Public Relations.)

Right: Russell Hall is one of three high-rise dormitories that the university built during its period of rapid expansion in the sixties and seventies. Russell can house just over a thousand residents; nearby Brumby and Creswell can accommodate about a thousand people each. (Photograph by Walker Montgomery, courtesy of the Office of Public Relations.)

242

Facing page, above: Founded in 1945, the Georgia Museum of Art resided in this building on north campus from 1958 until the opening of its new east campus facility in 1996. Constructed in 1904, this building served as the university's library until 1953; a lengthy remodeling preceded the museum's move into the building, and it later underwent yet another series of changes to ready it for a new life as one of the university's central administration offices. (Photograph by Walker Montgomery, courtesy of the Office of Public Relations.)

Above: In January 1983 a new governor assumed office in Atlanta, and once again he was a graduate of the University of Georgia. Lester Maddox and Jimmy Carter never attended the university, but most of the other governors of the state have been Georgia graduates, especially in the twentieth century. Here from right to left stand the outgoing governor, George Busbee (B.B.A. 1949, LL.B. 1952); Governor Joe Frank Harris (B.B.A. 1958); Elizabeth Harris; and Joe Frank Harris, Jr. (class of 1986). Rosalynn Carter stands just behind Harris. (Photograph courtesy of Sam Walton and the Red and Black.)

244

Facing page: The art department has grown steadily since Lamar Dodd took over its direction in 1938. The department offers courses in painting, sculpture, fabric and graphic design, jewelry and metal work, ceramics, and printmaking. (Photograph from the Pandora.)

Above: The University Symphony Orchestra performs under the direction of Professor Thomas Weaver, conductor from 1975 to 1982. The orchestra presents concerts on campus and also performs frequently throughout the state. (Photograph from the Pandora.)

Facing page: Traffic struggles up Baxter Street hill after a snowfall.· Athens, like most southern cities, is ill equipped to deal with even a few inches of snow. Most people stay at home and enjoy themselves until the snow begins to melt—usually just as soon as the sun appears. At the left of the photograph the edge of Brumby Hall marks the end of the campus while to the right the city's twin water towers loom over a hodgepodge of small businesses, mostly fast-order restaurants serving the students. (Photograph from the 1979 Pandora.)

Above: A snowstorm hits Athens, sending the students out for snowballing and sledding. (Photograph from the Pandora.)

Right: The best place for concentrated study (and quiet breaks) is the Main Library. After a long history of inadequate library facilities, the university made rapid progress in the 1960s and now boasts outstanding manuscript and book collections for graduate and undergraduate work. (Photograph from the Pandora.)

Left: A band reinforced by a pair of amplifiers begins the festivities at the Pi Kappa Phi House on South Milledge Avenue after a home football game against the Kentucky Wildcats. (Photograph from the Pandora.)

Left: A graduate of Boys' High School in Atlanta, Norman H. Giles became an internationally known authority in genetics at Yale. When he and his research team moved to Georgia in 1972, the university acquired its third member of the National Academy of Sciences. Here Professor Giles works in the Department of Molecular and Population Genetics within the Division of Biological Sciences. (Photograph by Walker Montgomery, courtesy of the Office of Public Relations.)

Right: The Special Collections Division of the University of Georgia Libraries houses rare books and manuscripts and also the photographic collection that furnished so many illustrations for this book. Shown here examining a tiny selection of the millions of individual items in the archives are, left to right, Robert M. Willingham, Jr. (M.A. 1972), curator of rare books; Kenneth Coleman (A.B. 1938, M.A. 1940), professor emeritus of history; Susan B. Tate (A.B. 1930, M.A. 1938), retired manuscript librarian; and F. N. Boney, professor of history. (Photograph by Walker Montgomery, courtesy of the Office of Public Relations.)

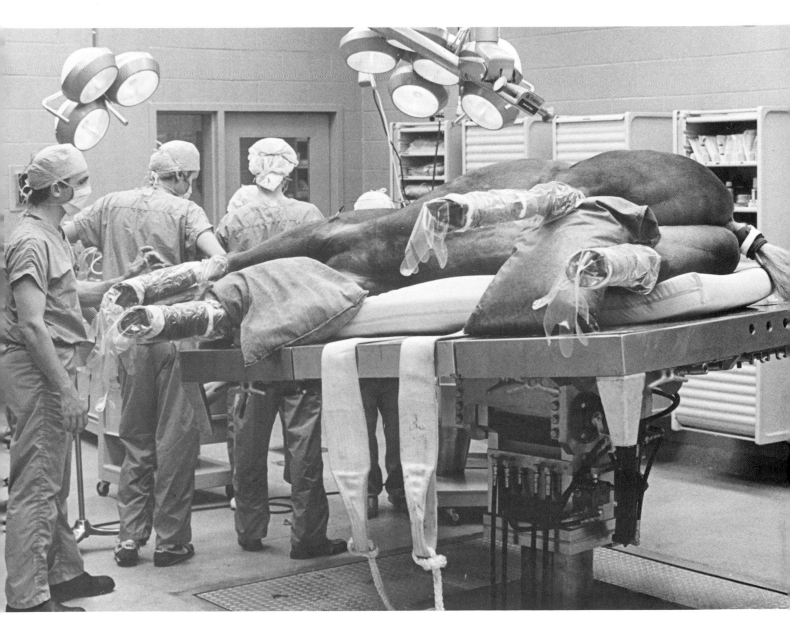

Facing page: Professor Glenn Burton of the College of Agriculture's Coastal Plains Experiment Station at Tifton is internationally known for his development of a hybrid pearl millet grain that has greatly increased food production, especially in India and Africa, and improved livestock production in the South and in tropical countries. His bermudas for turf cover many golf courses and football fields, including Sanford Stadium. A native of Nebraska who came to work at the University of Georgia in 1936 after completing his studies at Rutgers, Burton was made a member of the prestigious National Academy of Sciences in 1975. Then, in 1983 President Ronald Reagan awarded him the National Medal of Science. Here he chats with a television reporter in experimental fields at Tifton. (Courtesy of the College of Agriculture Experiment Stations.)

Above: The first veterinary medicine school at Georgia began in 1918 in three small buildings near Conner Hall, but in 1933 it ceased to exist. The success and steady growth of today's veterinary program owes much to Thomas J. Jones, who helped lead its revival in the post–World War II years and served as dean of the school until 1964. He was succeeded by Fred C. Davison, who became president of the university in 1967. The College of Veterinary Medicine on the south campus has one of the university's most elaborate physical plants with sophisticated facilities like this operating room for large animals. (Courtesy of the College of Veterinary Medicine.)

Facing page, above: Completed in 1832, the Chapel replaced an earlier wooden structure. The Arch did not appear until the 1850s, so the Chapel early became the main symbol of the university. (Photograph by Walker Montgomery, courtesy of the Office of Public Relations.)

Facing page, below: The University of Georgia Botanical Garden occupies a three-hundred-acre tract beside the Oconee River. The garden contains a representative collection of plants that grow in the Piedmont area. Its rose garden is a delightful spot to spend a sunny afternoon, and there are several miles of woodland trails for walkers. Shown here is the Callaway Building, the original main structure at the garden. It serves as administrative headquarters and houses offices as well as teaching, research, conference, and reception facilities. (Courtesy of the Office of Public Relations.)

Above: Built on Prince Avenue by John Thomas Grant in 1856, this fine Greek Revival mansion was bought after the Civil War by Benjamin Harvey Hill, a university graduate and prominent politician. The W. C. Bradley Foundation of Columbus presented it to the university in 1949. Extensively repaired, renovated, and landscaped, it now serves as the home of the president of the university. (Photograph by Al Wise, courtesy of the Office of Public Relations.)

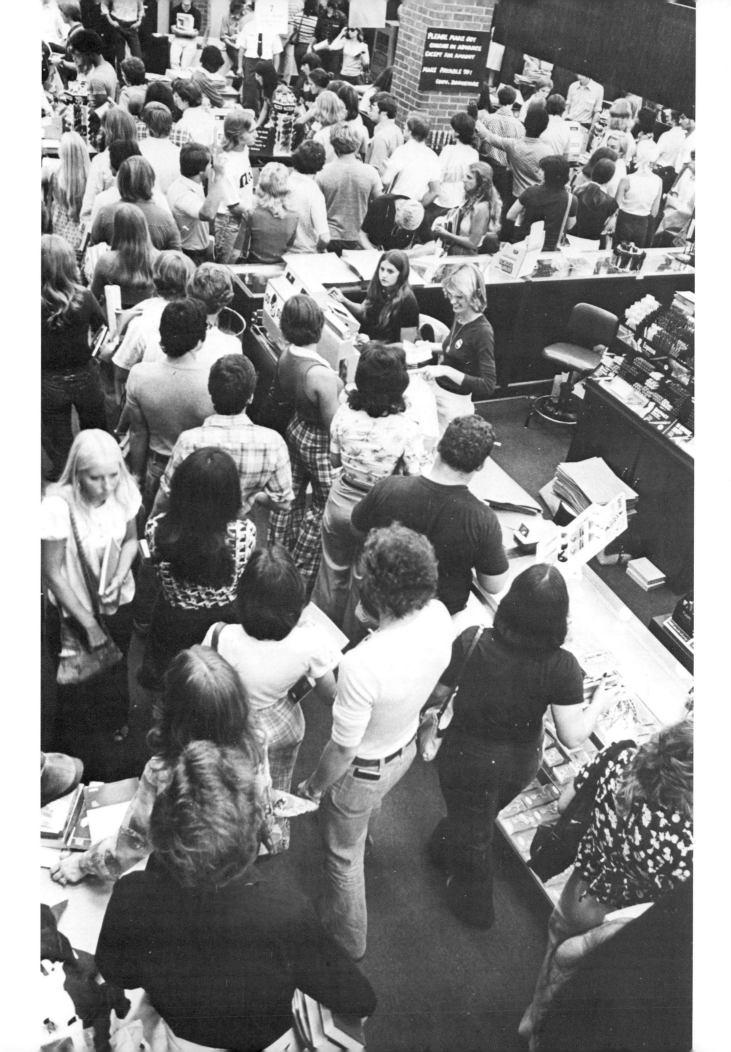

Facing page: Even early in the twentieth century when enrollment was less than a thousand, students complained about the confusion of registering for courses, paying fees, and getting books. Here students wait in endless lines to pay for their books at the beginning of the quarter. (Photograph from the *1981* Pandora.)

Above: The University of Georgia Redcoat Band performs at the half of a football game at Sanford Stadium. Over the years the uniforms and routines have varied, but the marching band remains a major organization on the campus. (Photograph from the Pandora.)

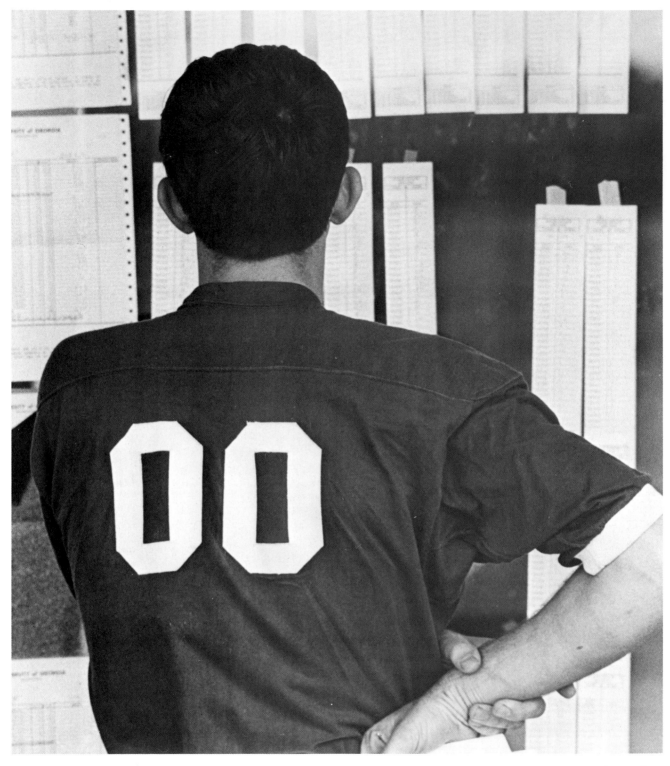

Above: Until fairly recently most teachers posted their quarter's grades for the benefit of those students who (for whatever reason) could not wait until the grades were mailed home. Here an anxious student scans the list. (Courtesy of the Office of Public Relations.)

Facing page: On a sunny day students take a break on the lawn in front of Park Hall, home of the English, classics, and comparative literature departments. (Photograph by Walker Montgomery, courtesy of the Office of Public Relations.)

Today and Tomorrow, 1985–1999

Fueled by a booming Georgia economy and the wholehearted support of people of the state, the university continued to improve quantitatively and qualitatively. By 1985 over 25,000 students were enrolled, and the school enjoyed a year-long bicentennial celebration of its chartering as the first state university. Appropriately enough Vice President of the United States George Bush (Yale, class of 1948) delivered the main address, reminding the proud southern school that its tap root ran back straight and true to Yale College in colonial Connecticut.

But the euphoria soon faded when a long-simmering dispute over tenure and retention exploded on campus, drawing national attention. Professor Jan Kemp of the Developmental Studies Program complained of special treatment for athletes, was terminated, took her case to Federal court, and won early in 1986, eventually receiving over a $1 million judgment. In the wake of this widely publicized struggle, President Fred C. Davison resigned, ending nineteen years of leadership in which the university had prospered as never before.

Hastily the Board of Regents found an interim president to preside over a school in some disarray. Henry King Stanford was a native Georgian, a graduate of Emory University who had gone on to earn a Ph.D. in political science from New York University. He had capped off his successful administrative career with nineteen years as president of the University of Miami, which had prospered much as Georgia had under Davison. Charging out of retirement in Americus, Stanford gave the university just the energetic and optimistic leadership it needed in a period of transition. No momentum had been lost when Charles B. Knapp began his ten-year administration in the summer of 1987.

A native of Iowa, Knapp earned a B.A. from Iowa State University in 1968 and M.A. and Ph.D. degrees in economics from the University of Wisconsin. He served as a special assistant to the Secretary of Labor under President Jimmy Carter and then attracted much attention as a wide-ranging executive vice president at Tulane University who guided a successful building program from 1982 to 1987.

At the University of Georgia he directed an even more ambitious building program that created the new east campus; almost overnight in the 1990s a whole new state-of-the-art complex of buildings emerged just across the railroad tracks from the south campus of science and technology. This brand new, third campus contained eight large new buildings of various uses, including a major commitment to the arts, which had long outgrown inadequate facilities on the original north campus. Certainly the Performing Arts Center and the Georgia Museum of Art were trailblazers, overshadowed only by the Ramsey Student Center for Physical Activities, the best such facility in the nation when it was completed in 1995.

On October 1, 1984, the University of Georgia began more than a year-long celebration of the two-hundredth anniversary of the chartering of the first state university in America. The high point of this convocation was a speech by Vice President of the United States George Bush, a Yale graduate who remembered the old bond: Yale the parent, Georgia the child. Since honorary degrees were not allowed then, Bush was made a fellow of the university, and President Fred C. Davison presented him with a sterling bicentennial medallion while Professor Thomas G. Dyer, General Chairman of the Bicentennial Celebration, and Vice President for Academic Affairs Virginia Trotter looked on. (Courtesy of the University of Georgia.)

Before Vice President George Bush's speech at the bicentennial convocation on October 1, 1984, hundreds of faculty members marched in a formal procession in the spacious Coliseum. When classes were first held at the university in 1801, university President Josiah Meigs was the entire faculty for a handful of students; on the eve of the Civil War four or five professors taught around a hundred students; and as late as 1900 around twenty professors taught less than 300 students. Then a slowly accelerating boom began, and by the bicentennial year of 1985 about 2,000 faculty directed over 25,000 students. The old school had come a long way, and it still had a long way to go. (Courtesy of the University of Georgia.)

A part of the bicentennial celebration was a large exhibition on the main floor of Memorial Hall. Lloyd Logan of the Art Department examined his handiwork, which showed the university's progress over two centuries in many different fields. Over a year later the exhibition was dismantled, and many of its components found permanent homes elsewhere on campus. This large area of Memorial Hall became a faculty dining hall, centrally located so that professors could conveniently meet for lunch. (Courtesy of the University of Georgia.)

In June 1997 Knapp concluded a decade of successful leadership at the university and accepted the presidency of the Aspen Institute, a think-tank in the nation's capital. Two months later a smooth transition was completed when Michael F. Adams assumed the presidency. A native southerner who attended public schools in Atlanta, Albany, Macon, and Chattanooga, he graduated from David Lipscomb College in Tennessee and then earned M.A. and Ph.D. degrees in political communications at Ohio State University in 1971 and 1973. While Georgia flourished under Knapp, Adams was providing similar leadership for Centre College, a small liberal arts school in Kentucky. Outgoing and energetic, he hit the ground running in Athens, and soon

selected Karen A. Holbrook, vice president for research and dean of the graduate school at the University of Florida, to become Georgia's new provost, in effect his chief executive officer in charge of day-to-day operation of the university.

The new administration soon moved to reorganize the academic structure of a school that had doubled in enrollment in a little over three decades, a period when many new fields and specialties emerged. In this booming thirty-year period, the university produced more alumni than it had in its entire previous existence, as the drive for national and international recognition continued without letup. For almost as long, no major new dormitories had been built, and the new presi-

On January 27, 1985, exactly two hundred years after his charter of the University of Georgia was enacted by the state legislature, the image of founder Abraham Baldwin appeared on campus in the hallway of the Fine Arts Building. Ms. Gladys McLelland, a town volunteer, and Chet Malanowski, manager of auxiliary services, presided at the first-day-of-issue sale of Baldwin's seven-cent commemorative stamp, while campus architect David Matheny and Ron North of the Institute of Natural Resources waited to make their purchases. Georgia Senator Baldwin died in Washington in 1807, but in a sense he never really left his beloved university—and never will. (Courtesy of the University of Georgia.)

dent championed on-campus living for undergraduates, not just in Athens but also on the university's growing overseas campuses at Cortona and Verona, Italy; Avignon, France; and Oxford, England.

Most of the school's physical facilities were strained by the burgeoning enrollment, which topped 30,000 in 1998 as the university prepared to celebrate the bicentennial of the beginning of classes in 1801, the same year that Thomas Jefferson became the third president of the nation. Plans to expand enrollment even further ensured that the campus building boom would continue.

As Georgia became a better and better school, it attracted more and more applicants, leading to steadily rising admission standards. Alumnus Zell Miller (A.B. 1957, M.A. in history 1958) played a major role in this steady improvement while governor from 1991–1999. All of the large profits from his new state lottery were poured into improving education at all levels, and a sizable proportion went into his new HOPE program (forged with President Knapp and other educators and passed into law in 1993). Georgians who brought a B average from high school and maintained it at any public college in the state received funds to cover tuition and books, and those who elected to attend a private college within the state received somewhat lesser support under the same conditions. Thus many more young Georgians stayed in-state for their higher education, and the university attracted many of the best of them, including Robert M. Sutherland, Scott Hershovitz, and Beth Shapiro, who ran the school's total of Rhodes scholars to eighteen.

The faculty won even more national recognition. Recently Susan R. Wessler (botany) and Lois K. Miller (entomology) increased the number of members in the prestigious National Academy of Sciences to nine, and five of these—Wyatt W. Anderson, John C. Avise, and Norman H. Giles (genetics); Overton Brent Berlin (anthropology); and Eugene P. Odum (ecology)—belonged to the similarly prestigious American Academy of Arts and Sciences. This preponderance of scientists was somewhat balanced by Professor Edward J. Larson (history and law), who won the 1998

On September 2, 1985, at half-time of the opening football game, Herschel Walker's number 34 was retired. He was joined by three other Georgia backs who had received the same honor. Walker led his team to a national championship as a freshman, won the Heisman Trophy as a junior, and then had a long, successful career in the pros.

In 1957 Theron Sapp (40) scored Georgia's most famous touchdown in a 7–0 victory over Georgia Tech that broke an eight year losing streak in that bitter rivalry. He was also all-conference and enjoyed success in the pros. Charley Trippi (62), probably the best all-round player in Bulldog history, won almost every honor but the Heisman and captained the undefeated and untied team of 1946. His professional career was equally outstanding, and in 1968

he was inducted into the pro Hall of Fame. Frank Sinkwich (21) won Georgia's first Heisman in 1942, playing alongside Trippi, and capped off his collegiate career by leading Georgia to a 9–0 win over U.C.L.A. in the Rose Bowl that same year. Then he won all-pro honors with the Detroit Lions in 1943–1944. (Courtesy of the University of Georgia Athletic Association.)

After nineteen years as president of the University of Miami, Henry King Stanford had earned a comfortable retirement, but in 1986 the Georgian assumed the presidency of the University of Georgia in a period of much change and some turmoil. Optimistic and energetic, he steered a steady course until Charles B. Knapp took over in 1987. In 1992 he returned to a grateful university to unveil his official portrait. (Courtesy of the University of Georgia.)

Opened in 1985, the Alice Hand Callaway Visitor Center and Conservatory replaced the original wooden Callaway Building as the main focus of the State Botanical Garden of Georgia, which is a little over a mile from the main campus. This modern structure soars out of the red clay like a magical crystal palace and hosts all manner of

events and festivities. The Cecil B. Day Chapel, the Garden Club of Georgia State Headquarters, and garden areas have also emerged as part of the booming, 313-acre facility designed to serve the whole state. (Courtesy of the University of Georgia.)

Pulitzer Prize in history for his innovative study of the famous Scopes monkey trial in Tennessee.

Clearly the old school in Athens was flourishing, but crucial events also occurred in Atlanta, where the central Board of Regents gradually expanded its power over the whole state higher education system, especially after it brought in a young, aggressive new chancellor in 1994. Stephen R. Portch was born and raised in England. He capped off his education with an M.A. and Ph.D. in English from Penn State University. He had eighteen years of administrative experience in the Wisconsin state system, so just as Chancellor Hill had looked to the University of Wisconsin when he upgraded Georgia at the beginning of the century, now the Regents turned to Wisconsin for leadership.

More and more money poured into the system, including consistent faculty raises, which allowed the University of Georgia to continue to recruit promising young scholars and outstanding senior scholars from all over the nation and sometimes the far corners of the world. In 1998 the whole system, the university included, switched from a quarter to a semester system, placing it more in harmony with the rest of the nation. The University of Georgia, Georgia Tech in Atlanta, and the medical college in Augusta remained the premier schools in the system, but many other colleges were assigned university status and Georgia State in Atlanta and Georgia Southern in Statesboro made dramatic progress.

Though not as often called the "flagship" of the

whole system as in the past, the university still blazed the trail for the whole state in academics and also in athletics. Football remained king, but for a few years after the Jan Kemp affair the school's academic requirements for athletes exceeded the N.C.A.A. standard, and the gridiron Dawgs slipped down a notch in the powerful Southeastern Conference. Even so Herschel Walker was joined in the pros by a stream of top-flight Dawg running backs including Rodney Hampton, Garrison Hearst, Robert Edwards, and

Terrell Davis of the Denver Broncos. But the most famous recent footballer was Bill Goldberg, a defensive tackle in the late 1980s who played awhile in the pros and then became a superstar in the wild and wooly world of professional wrestling. In 1996 Jim Donnan came from Marshall University and soon had Georgia football back in the upper echelon of the conference where it had traditionally competed.

Other men's teams did well too. The tennis squad always ranks high, and its excellent facilities draw the N.C.A.A. tournament to Athens almost every spring. Local (and very vocal) fans furnish additional incentive. And in May 1999 the tennis Dogs won the national title on their home court, gaining this honor for the third time. The basketball team had some good years, and in 1995 Coach Tubby Smith began a new dynasty before he moved on to Kentucky to win a national title. In 1990 the baseball team won the national title, and President Bush, once captain and first baseman at Yale, entertained the Diamond Dawgs at the White House. Coach Jack Bauerle forged a national powerhouse swimming team at the new Ramsey Center, the golf team improved steadily and won the national championship in June 1999, and all men's varsity teams remained competitive within the tough Southeastern Conference.

The burgeoning new field of women's varsity athletics did just as well. Athletic Director Vince Dooley and Assistant Athletic Director Liz Murphey adjusted to the demand for gender equality by shifting funds and hiring talented new coaches. The most dramatic success came in gymnastics with the arrival of Suzanne Yoculan in 1984. She soon established Georgia as a perennial powerhouse by winning five national titles. The fourth win in 1998 led to another White House reception. Coach Andy Landers compiled an outstanding record in basketball, coming close to a national title on several occasions. In golf and tennis the women consistently did well, and in March 1999 at the Ramsey Center, Coach Bauerle's women swimmers and divers, led by world-class breaststroker Kristy Kowal, convinc-

In 1990, Coach Steve Webber's Diamond Dawgs beat Oklahoma State 2–1 in the College World Series to take the national championship—Georgia's first ever in baseball. Here, the victors mob the infield after the final out of the game. Later that summer, President George Bush (who in 1985, as Vice President, helped the university celebrate its bicentennial), hosted the winning team at the White House. Bush had captained Yale's baseball team as an outstanding first baseman; once again the old Yale-Georgia connection resurfaced. (Courtesy of University of Georgia Athletic Association.)

ingly won the N.C.A.A. national championship. By then the fine women's soccer team was playing in a small, new stadium off Milledge Avenue near the Botanical Garden and the women's softball team was competing on their new field nearby, joining volleyball and track to round out the women's program.

A variety of club sports like lacrosse and rugby, and a large intramural program completed a huge athletic operation within a state committed to athletics at every level. From sandlots to Y and little leagues to high school competition and on to professional athletics spearheaded by the football Falcons, basketball Hawks, and baseball Braves, the state championed sports in general

and football in particular, and nowhere was the focus more intense and more successful than at the University of Georgia. It was altogether appropriate that the mastermind behind the 1996 Olympics in Atlanta was lawyer Billy Payne, a star end under Coach Dooley in the late 1960s, and that a worldwide audience could watch volleyball, rhythmic gymnastics, and soccer on the Athens campus. Certainly old Sanford Stadium has seen nothing more dramatic than the American soccer women's 2 to 1 championship victory over China, which was witnessed by the largest on-the-scene and TV audience ever to see a women's athletic event.

And so the university begins its third century surging forward on all fronts, supported by re-

Early in 1991 demonstrations against the Gulf War began on campus. Almost a dozen small, makeshift tents emerged near Phi Kappa Hall and Broad Street, and some rallies and heated debates followed. Unlike the movement in the Vietnam era, this antiwar movement enlisted only very limited student support and soon faded away. The university recognized the demonstrators' right to speak out in protest; they in turn maintained reasonable order, and soon everything returned to normal. (Photo by Don Nelson, courtesy of Don Nelson. Photo first published in the Athens Observer.)

268

Every late summer before the beginning of classes Vice President for Services and Outreach Gene Younts conducts a tour of Georgia for some of the new faculty. Usually 45 to 50 are available for this five-day trip through the geographically largest state east of the Mississippi River. From the mountains through

Atlanta to the former Civil War P.O.W. camp at Andersonville to the Agrirama at Tifton and on to Savannah and Skidaway Island and then the huge nuclear Plant Vogle and finally back to Athens, the newcomers are shown many things that many native Georgians have

not seen. Here in 1994 on the first day at Dahlonega in northwestern Georgia where an early gold rush began in 1829, Younts (head in front of post) joins the newcomers in panning for gold nuggets at the Consolidated Gold Mine Company. (Courtesy of Gene Younts.)

sources undreamed of during most of its existence and moving steadily upward in the hierarchy of American higher education. More and more optimistic, eager for new challenges, it stands taller than ever before. The ancient charter still whispers of duty to "the rising hope of our land" (the younger generations) and the Redcoat Band still blares "Glory, Glory to Old Georgia" and the sun still seems to shine brighter in old Athens

town. In the forefront of a state on the march, the old school, chartered over two centuries ago, has seen incredible change over the years, but it still remains true to its original (and slightly modernized) motto: "To teach, to serve, and to inquire into the nature of things." The long struggle is surely a success story, but the best is yet to come.

Above: In 1996 diver Jenny Rogers prepared to plunge from the ten-meter platform into the twenty-five-yard-wide, seventeen-foot-deep diving well. Behind her is the fifty-meter pool with a moveable bulkhead. She is facing a smaller recreational pool. This magnificent Gabrielson Natatorium (known locally as "the big swimming pool") helped the men's and women's swim teams become national powers, and it is the heart of the huge Ramsey Student Center for Physical Activities, completed in 1995. The Center also contains a 10,000-square-foot strength and conditioning room, ten racquetball and two squash courts, a one-eighth mile rubberized jogging track, eight courts for basketball and other games, a forty-four-foot climbing wall, a practice arena for gymnastics, and many other large rooms, plus classrooms and offices. (Courtesy of the University of Georgia.)

Facing page, bottom: Older buildings require constant upkeep and repair. Occasionally small fires erupted, but only once did major damage occur. Brooks Hall, designed by the famous architect Neel Reid, was completed in 1928 and enlarged considerably in 1972 as the Terry College of Business grew. In the blazing heat of the afternoon of August 14, 1995, welders replacing the roof accidentally started a fire that soon raged out of control. Finally firefighters from Athens and neighboring counties extinguished it, but the venerable old building had suffered extensive damage and did not return to full-time service until January 1997. (Courtesy of the University of Georgia.)

Below: Seemingly overnight, like springtime kudzu, a large new east campus sprang up in 1995. The upper third of the photograph shows the south campus with Stegeman Coliseum and Aderhold Hall standing tall and Sanford Stadium far in the distance. East Campus Road and the railroad track are mostly concealed by a line of trees. Below them sprawls the brand new campus, dominated by the huge Ramsey Student Center for Physical Activities, built at a cost of over $40 million and the best such facility in the nation when it opened in September 1995. To the right

stands a large parking deck. In the upper right stand three more new, state-of-the-art structures: (from right to left) the School of Music Building, the Performing Arts Center, and the Georgia Museum of Art. At the bottom the Four Towers Barn was undergoing extensive renovation. A few years after this photograph was taken, part of the small forest to the left was cleared to make way for the ultramodern University Health Center, and the open area to the right was filled in with a huge Animal Science Complex. By then the road system was completed and landscaping was well underway on the east campus, which continues to grow. (Courtesy of the University of Georgia.)

271

Director William U. Eiland conducts a tour in the impressive new Georgia Museum of Art, which opened in the spring of 1996. For over four decades it had remained cramped in the old library building on the north campus, but now it is one of the top academic museums in the nation with excellent facilities to house its 7,000 permanent works and the many traveling exhibitions that increasingly pass through Athens, Georgia. (Courtesy of the University of Georgia.)

The new Performing Arts Center on the new east campus is a state-of-the-art structure that contains two acoustically superior auditoriums, the 360-seat Ramsey Concert Hall and the 1,100-seat Hodgson Concert Hall, shown here brand new and awaiting its first perfor-mance. On April 14, 1996, this larger facility was packed for the grand opening as Distinguished Visiting Professor of Music Yoell Levi conducted the University Symphony Orchestra and Oratorio Chorus. After many years in crowded and makeshift quarters on the old north campus, music and art could finally flower in their new environment. (Courtesy of the University of Georgia.)

Above: The Four Towers Barn was completed in 1937 as one of the smaller campus construction projects funded by the federal government before America entered World War II. Eventually the central area was converted to office space for the College of Agriculture. In June 1996, just before the Olympics, the south end was made into a modern Visitors Center, and in August 1998 the north end was made into a student and alumni activities center for the College of Agricultural and Environmental Sciences (renamed in 1991). The landscaping around these end areas illustrates the overall beautification that has transformed the appearance of the university in recent years. (Courtesy of the University of Georgia.)

Facing page, bottom: Since 1940 the George Foster Peabody Awards have been administered by the Henry W. Grady College of Journalism and Mass Communication, and nothing projects the University of Georgia more onto the national scene than the annual luncheon in New York City in the spring when excellence in radio and television is recognized. On May 12, 1996, Telecommunications Professor Barry Sherman, director of the program, presented thirty-one awards, including one to Edith Ann's Christmas (Just Say Noell), a television drama in which Lily Tomlin played the leading role and also served as co-executive producer. (Courtesy of the University of Georgia.)

Above: On July 15, 1996, the Olympic torch relay passed through Athens. Here Teresa Edwards and Katrina McClain pass in front of the newly renamed Stegeman Coliseum, which was draped in Olympic regalia after being refurbished to host events in rhythmic gymnastics and women's volleyball. All-Americans on Georgia's perennially powerful women's basketball teams, Edwards and McClain had gone on to star in professional basketball as well on America's medal-winning Olympic women's basketball teams: Edwards four times and McClain three times. (Courtesy of University of Georgia Athletic Association.)

Appropriately, Vince Dooley and Billy Payne were among the torchbearers for the Olympic flame's journey through Athens. From 1964–1988 Dooley led Georgia football to new heights, and since 1979 as athletic director he has built one of the most successful overall programs in the nation. Payne starred at end under Coach Dooley in the late 1960s, graduated from the university's law school, and practiced successfully in Atlanta for many years before he emerged as the leader of that city's long-shot, but ultimately successful, bid to host the 1996 Olympics. (Courtesy of the University of Georgia.)

After his stint in the Olympic torch run, University President Charles B. Knapp stood with his wife Lynne before the new Memorial Wall in Olympic Plaza in front of Stegeman Coliseum. With the Knapps is retired professor of art John D. Kehoe, founder and longtime director of the University of Georgia Studies Abroad Program at Cortona, Italy.

Kehoe designed the massive, five-faceted marble wall which will forever remind visitors of a glorious Olympic summer in Athens. On the front it lists five universal passions (awe, anguish, love, triumph, and joy) in English, Chinese, Classical Greek, Hindi, Swahili, German, Arabic, French, Japanese, Spanish, and Russian. On the back it records forty-eight University of Georgia men and women who have performed in the modern Olympics beginning in 1936 (including some repeaters), and wisely it leaves plenty of space for future performers. (Courtesy of the University of Georgia.)

With the old hedges temporarily removed to make way for the broader soccer field, Sanford Stadium hosted the final rounds of Olympic soccer in the summer of 1996. A capacity crowd of 86,117 witnessed the men's team from Nigeria upset Argentina, but the most dramatic contests featured a determined American women's team that defeated Norway 2 to 1 on July 28 before 64,196 fans and then on August 1 won the gold medal by beating China 2 to 1 as 76,481 spectators roared their approval. Since 1929 old Sanford Stadium had witnessed many dramatic Dawg triumphs, but nothing matched the emotion of this all-American victory. (Courtesy of University of Georgia Athletic Association.)

Above: Gators, Tigers, Yellow Jackets, Wildcats, Volunteers, Gamecocks, and especially Bulldogs have tasted glory between the hedges at Sanford Stadium. But the most dramatic triumph of all occurred without the hedges as the U.S. women's soccer team won the Olympic gold medal in 1996 and carried Old Glory for a victory lap around the field as the crowd roared its delight. Many of

the victors were from the powerful University of North Carolina team and not one was from the University of Georgia, but old Georgia was never prouder. And soccer, especially for women and girls, blossomed in the Athens area. (Courtesy of the University of Georgia.)

Facing page, above: Just before the beginning of every academic year, the new faculty and many others are invited to a reception at the President's House, about a mile from the original north campus. This antebellum Greek Revival mansion stands as a reminder of the university's deep roots, and its formal downstairs and large, carefully landscaped backyard host many school functions. The new semester system pushed this party back into August as a new administrative team assumed command: (from left to right) Senior Vice President and Provost Karen A. Holbrook; President Michael F. Adams and his wife, Mary Ethridge Adams; and Acting Vice President for Instruction Thomas G. Dyer. (Courtesy of the University of Georgia.)

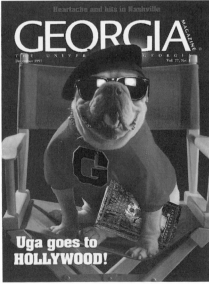

Left: The University of Georgia is the only major college that buries its mascots within its stadium, and someday UGA V will join his father and others in a cement vault. UGA IV attracted a lot of attention, especially when he accompanied Herschel Walker when he was awarded the Heisman trophy in New York in 1982. Now his son has become even more of a media sensation. UGA V appeared on the cover of Sports Illustrated *(April 28, 1997), which proclaimed him "No. 1 Mascot," and here on the cover of* Georgia Magazine *(December 1997) to remind his fans that he played a role in Clint Eastwood's movie* Midnight in the Garden of Good and Evil, *which was filmed in UGA's hometown of Savannah. His friend and owner, alumnus Frank W. "Sonny" Seiler, played a larger role in the same film. (Courtesy of* Athens Daily News *and* Athens Banner-Herald.*)*

Left: As soon as he graduated from Southwest DeKalb High School in Atlanta, young Quincy Carter entered the Chicago Cubs baseball organization, and three years later he became the Dawgs twenty-one-year-old freshman sensation at quarterback, leading the team to a 8 and 3 regular season with losses only to Florida, Georgia Tech, and Tennessee, the national champion, and capping off the 1998 season with a dramatic 35 to 33 victory over Virginia in the Peach Bowl. Carter was an all-round athlete and especially dangerous passer; the running attack was spear-headed by Olandis Gary, number 22, who came with Coach Jim Donnan from Marshall University and served as a team captain in 1998. (Photo by Philip Williams, Courtesy of University of Georgia Athletic Association.)

Below: Being one of the first black students to integrate the university in 1961 was not easy, but Charlayne Hunter-Gault became a staunch alumnus after graduating with a B.A. in journalism in 1963. She spoke at commencement in 1988, the twenty-fifth anniversary of her own graduation, attended the Holmes-Hunter lectures whenever her successful journalism career permitted, and on September 28, 1998, delivered the fourth prestigious Walter Barnard Hill lecture, where she joined President Michael F. Adams in celebrating the moment. Early in her career she wrote for the New York Times for a decade; then she appeared on the Public Broadcasting Service's MacNeil/Lehrer News Hour for years; and then she became National Public Radio's chief Africa correspondent, and in March 1999 signed on as C.N.N. International's bureau chief in Johannesburg, South Africa. (Courtesy of the University of Georgia.)

Left: Suzanne Yoculan, once a gymnast at Pennsylvania State University, came to Georgia in 1984 to begin her coaching career. Successful from the start, she led her women's team to dominance in the Southeastern Conference and a fifth national title by 1999. One of her top performers was All-American Karin Lichey, who, among her many triumphs, scored a perfect 40 against the University of Kentucky. Here she is congratulated by her coach and assistant coach Steve Ballard at the N.C.A.A. Southeastern Regionals in 1998. (Photo by Dwayne C. Bass, Courtesy of University of Georgia Athletic Association.)

Below: Edward J. Larson, Richard B. Russell Professor of History and Law, won the 1998 Pulitzer Prize for History for his book Summer for the Gods: The Scopes Trial and America's Continuing Debate over Science and Religion. *Over the years he also earned a reputation as an outstanding teacher, a combination often sought but not so often attained in American higher education. (Courtesy of University of Georgia.)*

Traditionally University of Georgia graduates have played a major role in state politics, and indeed they have often dominated that turbulent arena. A good example is Zell Miller, governor from 1991 to 1999. He received an A.B. in 1957 and a master's in history in 1958. Known as the "education governor" for his HOPE scholarship program and many other efforts at every level of public education, in July 1998 he was named a Distinguished Professor of Higher Education and the first holder of the Philip H. Alston Junior Chair. Alston graduated from Georgia in 1932 and became a prominent Atlanta businessman who served on the Board of Regents and performed many other services for his old university before his death in 1988. After a formal ceremony in the Chapel, the main participants walked to another old university symbol, the Arch. Left to right: Elkin Alston Cushman, John G. "Jimmy" Alston, and Elkin Goddard Alston (the children and widow of Philip H. Alston, Jr.), Governor and Mrs. Zell Miller, and Mrs. and President Michael F. Adams. (Courtesy of the University of Georgia.)

Since he took command of the whole University System of Georgia in 1994, Chancellor Stephen R. Portch has furnished vigorous leadership. Though based in Atlanta, he has traveled all over the state to every institution in the system, exchanging ideas with students and faculty. Early in December 1998 he chatted with student leaders in the Tate Center at the University of Georgia, still the leading school in the whole system. (Courtesy of the University of Georgia.)

Left: The university hosts all manner of guest speakers—everything from Nobel prize winners to show business celebrities. Indeed, students and professors can hardly keep up with the flood of experts who visit the campus. On March 29, 1999, Spike Lee, the famous movie actor and director, addressed a full house in the volleyball arena at the new Ramsey Center. (Courtesy of the University of Georgia.)

Below: Stretched along Baxter Street on the west campus stand the last three dormitories built when enrollment was roughly half of what it was in 1999 (from bottom to top): Creswell Hall (1963), Russell Hall (1967), and Brumby Hall (1966). To the left, a parking deck emerged in 1993. Even so, large healthy trees remain throughout the campus and town. New dormitories are being considered after a three-decade moratorium. (Courtesy of the University of Georgia.)

Especially for freshmen, moving into a campus dormitory is a real rite of passage, the beginning of a new life. It is also a real hassle. Packing everything but the family dog into a vehicle, hauling a big load to Athens, and then cramming it all into a room while a new roommate does the same thing makes for a busy and exciting day, one that sticks in the memory for a lifetime. (Courtesy of the University of Georgia.)

Signs of the times at large universities like Georgia are crowds and congestion. People, buses, and automobiles compete for control of Baldwin Street, a city thoroughfare that runs through the heart of the north campus. (Courtesy of the University of Georgia.)

287

As the university has grown steadily, parking has become more and more of a problem. Inevitably, huge, ungainly, but essential parking decks have sprung up all over the campus. The largest of all, holding 1,200 automobiles, emerged on the eastern edge of the old north campus, towering over East Campus Road–Thomas Street. (Courtesy of the University of Georgia.)

Facing page: Town and gown intermingle in downtown Athens across from the Arch. Restaurants, bars, bookstores, and all manner of small, specialty shops line Broad Street and extend several blocks northward into the growing city. Campus and city bus systems lengthen the students' reach to most areas of Athens-Clarke County, but the automobile still reigns supreme in this very American environment. (Courtesy of the University of Georgia.)

Above: Traditional lecture courses are now often reinforced by computers—or rows of computers—especially in the more modern classroom buildings. Here Professor Robert J. Vandenberg of the Terry College of Business assists undergraduates with the special facilities available in Caldwell Hall. (Courtesy of the University of Georgia.)

Facing page, bottom: All-everything at Rome High School in northwestern Georgia, Beth Alison Shapiro came to the University as a prestigious Foundation Fellow. She began as a journalism major in the honors program and soon switched to ecology. Shapiro did nine months of field work in Central America and compiled a straight 4.0 average in her regular class work. As in high school, she shined in many directions. Finally in 1999 Shapiro became the University of Georgia's eighteenth Rhodes Scholar (and the first woman at the university so recognized). She will study evolutionary and community ecology at Oxford University as she progresses toward a Ph.D. and an anticipated career of teaching and research at the university level. Remarkably, Shapiro was the third university student within a four year period to become a Rhodes Scholar. Scott Hershovitz, a political science and philosophy student, took the honors in 1998, and Robert Sutherland, who focused on conservation ecology and sustainable development, was named in 1996. (Courtesy of the University of Georgia.)

Above: Rallying outside Memorial Hall where much of their on-campus social life is centered, foreign students display the flags of their homelands or a friend's homeland. Over 3 percent of the student population hails from abroad. Asia and then Europe furnish the largest contingents, with New World neighbors like Canada, Brazil, and Colombia prominent, too. More are graduate students than undergraduates, and many more concentrate on the sciences than on the arts and humanities. Small contingents in the 1930s have grown into large groups who have a decided impact on the University. (Courtesy of Marcus J. Longmuir, International Student Life, University of Georgia.)

The university's libraries will never be completely free from the challenges of managing an avalanche of books and other documents within limited physical space. Significant help came along in 1995, however, with the launch of GALILEO (GeorgiA LIbrary LEarning Online). A cyberspace repository of knowledge and information, GALILEO gives schools, libraries, and other institutions around the state access to over 100 databases. GALILEO resources include full texts of more than 2,000 journals, an encyclopedia, business directories, government publications, and GIL (GALILEO Interconnected Libraries), a web-based online union catalog of all the book collections of the university system. At these termi-nals in the main library, where great banks of card catalogs once stood, students can access GALILEO, "wire" themselves into endless destinations around the world, or maybe just slip in a quick (but nonetheless frowned-upon) game of Minesweeper or Solitaire. (Courtesy of the University of Georgia.)

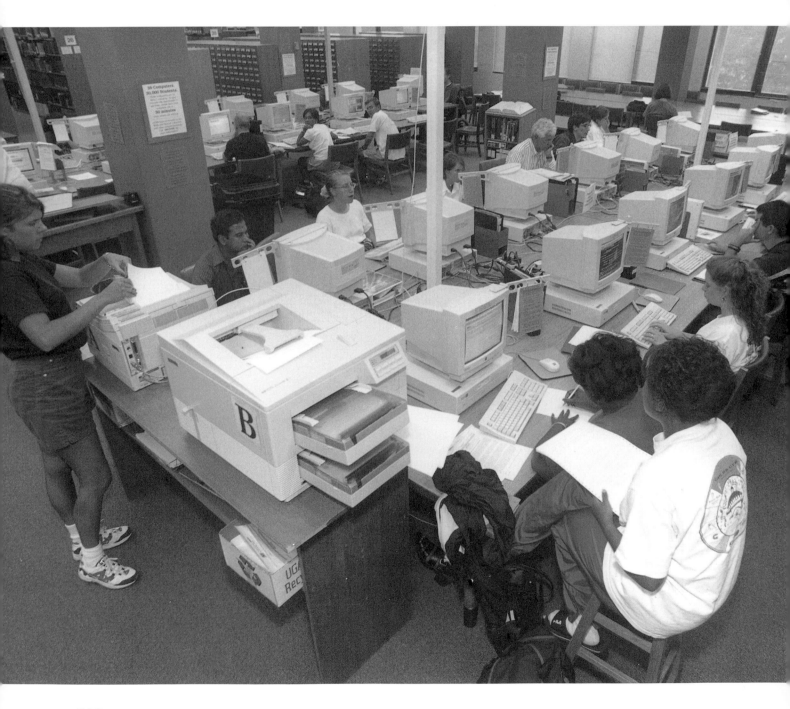

With renewed commitment of service to both its scholarly and general-interest readership, the University of Georgia Press entered its sixtieth year of publishing in 1999. Shown here celebrating this milestone, Director Karen Orchard (left of center) stands with other Press members and two authors, Wilbur H. *Duncan and Marion B. Duncan (both immediately right of Orchard). In the spring of 1999 the Press published the Duncans' long-awaited* Wildflowers of the Eastern United States *to much acclaim. (Courtesy of the University of Georgia Press.)*

Built in the backwoods of early Georgia in 1806, Old College housed the entire university for a few years and then served as a dormitory for the rest of the century. Now, like most other antebellum buildings on campus, it contains administrative offices. But students and faculty still gather on its beautifully maintained grounds, especially in the President's Club Garden where the names of major benefactors are engraved on the brick wall. Old College still reminds us that the past is only yesterday. (Courtesy of the University of Georgia.)

Bibliographical Note

On the third floor of the main library, the Hargrett Rare Book and Manuscript Library contains a complete run of the *Pandora* from its beginning in 1886 and the *Georgia Alumni Record* from 1920; the minutes of the Board of Trustees, the Board of Regents, and the faculty (with gaps); a fine collection of photographs, many letters, and other manuscripts of persons connected with the university; and all manner of peripheral material.

Major published works include A. L. Hull's *A Historical Sketch of the University of Georgia* (1894) and *Annals of Athens, Georgia, 1801–1901* (1906). E. Merton Coulter's lively and anecdotal *College Life in the Old South* (1928) deals only with the University of Georgia and runs through 1870. Thomas Walter Reed's voluminous "History of the University of Georgia" remains in nineteen typewritten volumes in the Hargrett Library, but a condensation was published in 1974 by Ray Mathis under the title *"Uncle Tom" Reed's Memoir of the University of Georgia*. Robert Preston Brooks's *The University of Georgia Under Sixteen Administrations: 1785–1955* (1956) is a useful factual summary, and F. N. Boney's *A Walking Tour of the University of Georgia* (1989) adds more detail. James K. Reap's *Athens: A Pictorial History* (1982) and Frances Taliaferro Thomas's *A Portrait of Historic Athens and Clarke County* (1992) blend the university into a larger community. Overall, the best study of the school is Thomas G. Dyer's *The University of Georgia: A Bicentennial History* (1985).

Index